IT IS THE DEVIL'S TURN TO SPEAK

THE DEVIL'S BIBLE

William Allan Lavey
Andreas Bathory

Descrierea CIP a Bibliotecii Naţionale a României
LAVEY, WILLIAM ALLAN
   The devil's bible / William Allan Lavey, Andreas Bathory. -
Iaşi : StudIS, 2018
   ISBN 978-606-775-903-7
I. Bathory, Andreas
II. Allan Lavey

Editura StudIS adicenter@yahoo.com
Iasi, Sos. Stefan cel Mare, nr.5 Tel./fax: 0232 – 217.754

A Coming Time of Great Change, Great Upheaval, and GREAT POWER!

A time of great change, the end of one era and the entrance of another. Unbeknownst to many is the reality that is felt by all! it doesn't take the center of a spotlight to take the hint that everyone is sensitive to the presentation of coming great changes in our midst! A Pope who reaches out to all and most importantly to those tradition has overlooked is a prime example of the rising spirit that is seeking dominance at a time when so many of the forces of the Shadow seek disconnection! Trust yourself! Manners and traditions in belief matter not! Construct, footwork, and expression does! Take care to not warp or to thwart otherwise well-meant intents of the many spirits around you!

Tumult and upheaval leading to new paths and emerging wonder. Yes, schedules and interplay between figures and minds alter rivers of dates and dawns. Instead of seeking out and struggling to try and lock down the "when's", live and work instead toward clarity as to the "why's!"

"Much is coming, much has come, but what still remains, is what has yet to be done!"

If you struggle to gain insight and intuition into what lies ahead, don't micro-manage the particulars of the sage and the prophet, regardless of theirs or your cross, crux, or your own compendium; every way will carry vision and dawning insight!

All you need to be concerned with is your own connection, your own soul's connection and making it clear to you! Then will come the insights you seek regarding your own path, your own future in life, and your opportunity as well as in warning!

The vestiges of wisdom and understanding from both the past and to those who were our past call to us! How many have ears and spirits through which to gain insight and intuition, but who still choose to never understand! What comes now for you individually and we collectively as a gathering of souls is the sum of that which is understood by some, though felt by all!

Where Penemue casts wisdom and understanding, it is frequently overlooked and taken as parchment for none, where to dissuade oneself of the calling of any particular path, your own path that is calling! It's akin to becoming sure of all while also of nothing in return. Doubt not your abilities and the calling of your path! Doubt rather the assertions of those who attempt to convince you of a wisdom that seeks to sway you off and out of your own way.

It is usually those stalwarts who hold true in many and any way who abiding the passages of time, are also eventually recognized as being sure, and right, and true to not only themselves, but of many in return.

William Allan Lavey & Andreas Bathory

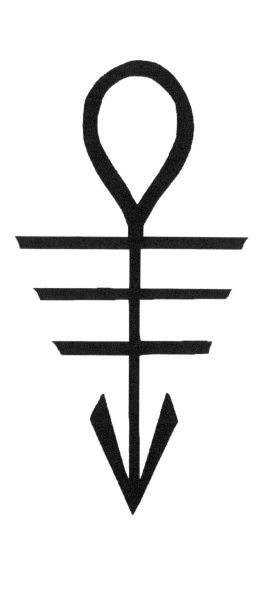

A Train in Wait

There's a train in wait just before the veil to take you along our way, it heads for stops, some odd, some tops, and wayward it stops where we'll stay. Far along the line and the rock turns to vine, and the brick over plaining grassy mane, we may draw up its cue, and then stop where we'd do, here and there, by and where could call our play. As the trip makes its drops and ponder should be walk, we could bid any adieu that called our pic, but remember as you do, as you want to travel through, that this train of yours will never, ever, mock! You go where you wish, we yearn for what we yearn, and in the end, its ALWAYS our destiny that is the marker on our Magick ticket! A calm, peaceful, and an illuminating night!

ABSOLUTELY REFUSE TO GIVE UP!

I felt it not only necessary but incredibly prudent to share this piece in my BLOG today! Why?

It's simple really...

This really is where that age old, fabled, and legendary MAGICK OF OUR DETERMINED SPIRIT ORIGINATES!

This and the fact that this is me to a "T", and along with so many others I see, all together we rise back up again and again and collectively in a purely stoic fashion we REFUSE TO GIVE UP come Hell or the tides of more discontent!

In this way those of us who have lived this surely know that our path is right and true. For who else in their right mind would put up with all of this if they didn't still behold a positive vision of their fellows and of all the world to be as true? I mean really! Think about it for a minute...

Ah Intelligence...

And intelligence,... while certainly a fascination for many who would try and articulate what they perceive as "the mind", it not being a number, a value, a prime parable in a box, is nothing more than simply the soul flexing itself through the creative extensions of the tendrils of the spirit upon all of our surrounding perspectives of creation! Hence, why they are so intertwined like ivy along a trellis.

All too many people who have sought to nickel and dime the real meaning behind this hypothetical construct have served it well. Wechsler, Freud,

Skinner, and a host of other sages of the mind and the article of human behavior and habit. Where there was damage done due to this predilection with the value of humankind habit? Well, scores of culture and various segments of people have been played and there is no other way to describe it.

A long time ago when I was on the course of psychometric study of such various tools, it finally occurred to me that while these measures of habit and attention did indeed serve to classify in their own ways, they also dealt out judgments unworthy to so many others. This is when I began to have a falling out with the behaviorist school of thought with regard to people from all over the world and of any age group!

You see, where I finally ended up was to occupy the island of thought that spoke of unnerving the mind with the fixation upon having to quantify those world focused attentive and our many memory habits and to think of people in their true and proper terms, as the sole arbiters and negotiators of their souls. This remaining a thing never to be defined by any other person. Certainly never a social worker, a governmental status placer, or a workplace administrator.

The hypothetical construct that has always been attributed to that word, "intelligence" is no real thing at all and in its own way has perhaps done more to harm that it ever did to help! In fact, due to my experience both professionally and personally, I finally found that if anything could be said about this word, Einstein did perhaps say it best.

That thing we call intelligence is the soul flexing its creative expression!

Angelic Guardians

When you awaken and find yourself in the midst of a sudden torrent of storms and general upset, take refuge in the guardianship of the wings of your Angels who are always by our side!

By day they're your allies shoulder to shoulder they stand, by night they watch over you with their flame in their hands. Twilight shines of their beacons breaking through all the dark and as dawning sun rises you then follow their mark.

They are always supporting every footstep you take, every turn, every bend, every journey you make. Then when we all of our challenge seems beset by dark nets, hold your Angel's firm shoulder you will never regret!

There is nothing in creation that can break their soul-bond, and our need for their guidance, as your path seems prolonged. For that dawning will come when all storms have then passed, and your Angels still with us until days at their last!

BE "I AM EMPOWERED!"
Stop worrying about those people and those things that in your past occupied so many of your concerns! The truth is that NONE OF THEM MATTER! The real trick isn't in proving that you are able to struggle against the erosive and the destructive elements of greed, degradation, and mediocrity that abound, but rather in being able to set them all quietly aside and focus your attention on ascending to that state of Mastery in your life that makes the rest positively irrelevant! Then is when you will find yourself standing at the pinnacle of a state of wonder where NOBODY and NOTHING can alter your essence!!!
Along the path of life today it's an almost instinctive habit where we non-consciously acquiesce to the vaguely adopted perception that the impact that the world and that others have upon our lives are more deterministic than they actually are! The truth is that we empower others just as much as we choose to, point, done, and exclamation!

Sometimes we forget that as we try to keep up our pace with our perceptions of life and modern civilization that not everything we feel, experience, and create is absolutely dependent upon a mechanized and rote passage of simply doing in life by direction. Unfortunately we've become habituated and in many ways enwrapped into the belief system that who we are and what we are is almost entirely relegated to the vestiges of the tides of "other-than-ness" instead of centering ourselves in the empowered reality of ABSOLUTELY and ENTIRELY commanding our own destiny!

This is what I'm describing as being "I AM!"

In order to change these rogue misperceptions in our minds and their accompanying emergence in the reality along our path of life, we must start by changing how we initially allow ourselves to think of our own power, and then commanding our thoughts to veer us away from even hinting that others, ANY OTHERS, hold any power or sway upon or over us! If we finally use this as a starting point from where to then set a new waypoint for our emerging successes and our affluent futures;

THEN EVERYTHING WILL BEGIN TO CHANGE FOR US!

Don't doubt it!

DO IT!

Become "I AM EMPOWERED", instead of allowing yourself to be a follower!

Bothered by a Sudden Silence Within?
I've noticed a trend recently that seems to be bothering an increasing number of fellow path walkers. One that I can certainly appreciate and have gone through myself, and so, I thought to share just a bit hoping that it might help someone else out there.
Look,... There are down periods and times for everyone. Every seer, every active spiritualist, every psychic medium, and yes for every Witch, Priestess, High Priest/Priestess, and every spiritual servant from every possible form of faith and belief. When the path becomes suddenly subtle and the mirror of our inner vision and the power of soul and spirit seem to take a little breather for a bit, there are really only two better ways to process it.
One, could be that you're going through some sort of mis-alignment or some obscurity in your own "prism" so to speak. A hard fact to face, but if so, best we admit it and then re-align ourselves toot-sweet for our own good!

Another however could just be that there is a reason for the simmer on the waters of creation for you at the moment! A lot of visionaries take such times with a sense of frustration thinking themselves blinded or functioning in some sort of a lights out fashion. It's never easy to stomach, especially when you're the type of spirit who is used to being out there in the fray of the makings of life all of the time!

One of the things that over time I've had to come to terms with is that such times have their purpose even when in their midst we don't have the first clue as to why we feel as if we are suddenly sent to some form of proverbial Coventry.

The best way to endure these passages in our strength and vision is to take them in stride, an honest stride in humility! Perhaps the universe is giving you a break? Perhaps you have somehow sectioned yourself away from things for a while without even realizing it? Perhaps you have unconsciously veered your course to one side or the other in your own defense? Or, perhaps you are being prepared for something else, given a respite, allowed to fortify and refortify your spirit and soul for a coming tidal shift of immense proportions?

I recall a period of my life quite a long time ago when I found myself being suddenly and absolutely thrown into the face of an unplanned and rather unforeseen hail storm. It was the likes of which that tend to alter one's course and path forever.

What I would in time discover was that such a profound shift and change along the path frequently comes with its own storm and with its own following respite, and it did indeed alter my course drastically. In fact, it set up another literal "Golden Dawn" that for me, would carry great effects not only upon my own life and the power of my path, but also upon that of so many others around me.

Hey, let's face it! We are all in the midst of very trying, difficult, and tumultuous times in our lives and in our world right now! There are so many around us who are crying for answers, seeking direction, yearning for some explanation not to mention trying to get a grip on just where they might find some rationality for their safety and that of their loved ones.

Many try, most frequently in vain, to seek the example of their leaders and representatives. Not too many surprises there when such tend to come up dry? Many others choose the course of hunkering down and making pleas to creation itself to just have done with it all! Who wouldn't really!?

So, if you are a soul worker, a spirit seeker, a psychic medium, a practitioner of some form in the art of the spirit and the spirits, that of nature, in no matter what form of belief you follow and adhere to, and if you feel caught up in some desert of creation for a time, despair not!

Your time is coming! Your time WILL come!

One suggestion if it helps. Don't choose to suddenly think you've been all wrong and hastily alter the meaning of the shine of your spirit thus suddenly taking up some pixie dust path or any other way if such glitter doesn't necessarily suit you!

BE! Remain true to yourself and to your path!

It carries truth for you and it WILL serve you and continue to serve you well!

Choose the way of a withdrawal for a time and use it in benefit to gather your wits, to build your strengths, to better center your power, and to seek closer and clearer connections with those spirits, the angels, and/or the Gods who you connect to!

You are going to need such connections in the near future, most likely much sooner than you think!

Carry No Regrets

There is a great freeway that carries us all onward towards any destination we would so desire. It travels around any landscape, it traverses any and all possible avenues, and it carries us to any experience and tone or color of life we could ever want. The thing to remember however is, that it also advances an infinite number of exits for us that depending upon our decisions, arrives at places in life both wondrous and terrifying leaving the choices to all of our passages. This is the price of our journey along creations freeway and we tend to forget the presence of the free will that gives us the power to get there.

I've been spending a lot of time in reflections lately because of many various personal and professional changes that are taking place in my life, and it seems that I'm not all alone by some of the commentary that I've witnessed on the part of others. Times and periods of change tend to elicit reflection more than it might otherwise. In part due to the amount of energy we are focusing upon so many of the alternatives we face. In other regards however, there is a spirit of all that got us to where we find ourselves and why it is we are facing said changes.

. It's natural of course. Such periods instigate our deeper sources of insight where otherwise, most simply file them all away someplace deep and rather dusty.

It's a common place to yearn for that state of being where we may look back and not have bitter lessons staring us in our mind's eye. Forestalling any recitation of the actuary of the soul that carries such burdens, alas, such is the capacity of the beast that is the course of life.

In this as virtually every other soul in existence, I've come to have to accept in the best ways possible that I've never always made the best choices in my life. I've certainly had to come to accept I've made plenty of mistakes and will no doubt continue to along my way. This is the reason I refer to the "beast" of the course of life. It's not always predictable, wild in fact at times, even and especially for a psychic when so much of the freeway remains open and in the realm of the possible. One thing that I do know, is this...

To truly arrive at that place in life where we may finally open our eyes and look down in a sense of personal peace with ourselves is a longing that we all seek as a basic intuition for who and what we really are and where we truly came from before we set out upon this particular journey.

Arriving at this place insists upon several basic traits that we must agree with right down to the core of our soul, or else true peace will remain elusive.

One, is that we may finally live within the moment! Seek not always what is yet to be or what we pray may become! To live truly within the moment, from one moment to the next, will allow us to finally "BE" and to focus our energies upon this "BEING" and not expending so much of our constant energy on always "SEEKING!"

Two, is that we may set aside our resentments at last with others, ALL OTHERS! You see, when we live in a state of constant resentment, blaming others, setting anger as our guide, and most of all refusing to forgive ourselves, residing in a state of the NOW, in peace can never and will never be a real possibility.

Three, and perhaps the most difficult is to CARRY NO REGRETS about what has been, what was, all of what could have been, all of the mistakes, so many poor decisions, all of our hurts, the wrongs turns we've made, the bad people choices we fell into, all of the poor workplace decisions we acted upon, and of course the many friends who have for so many reasons left our lives, finally and truly!

If we carry no regrets any longer and accept ourselves as we are, not as we would rather be, then, is when, we may finally embrace the power and the strength that has always been sitting like ladies and gentlemen in waiting inside of us all!

Changes bring about great things within us.

Changes have the capacity to terrify us because of all of the unknowns.

When however we finally learn that we can never end up at any place, anytime, anywhere, other than there where we were always heading to begin with, is when we may better learn to embrace ourselves in our NOW!

This moment! Because now will never come again! Now is all there is!

Channeling Our Own Conduits of POWER AND SUCCESS in This Life!

With the Ravens call we greet the morn and look to daytime's strength, then wander forth toward evenings worth then embrace it all at length! Muster all your power and center well making all the world mark wise, your Magick mirth sets your path first before all marveled eyes!

With the tone of our spirit let's all begin to recognize that we are now entering an unrivaled period in the world and as a result, an unrivaled period in our own lives! We often look to those sources of our own understandings of the philosophy of life as we understand it to help us to navigate and set the brilliance of our days.

As we all now enter a dawning and long anticipated age of our common awareness, right along with it comes the tides of energy of our common spirit that do more than just signal what we have yet to create, but what we are creating right now!

You see, as we become aware that WE ARE THE CONDUITS OF POWER channeling our own sunrise, then we adopt and take ownership of our POWER!

Congruence! Bringing Us Back Into Alignment!

We effect, we project, we alter, we falter, we consign, we resign; everywhere we go and whatever we do we're affecting what we encounter with the force of our own presence! In order to maximize our potential however requires that we be unalterably congruent of our own essence!

Why?

In doing so, we are not only allowing ourselves to "BE" precisely who and what we truly are, but we are also then allowing ALL of creation to exert its powers through us!

When we mask ourselves off from our being, in any way, we are throwing off our own innate potential and placing ourselves way out of alignment with the way that we were actually meant to be!

Think of it as aligning a crystal in the light so that it perfectly focuses the force and strength of that light that shines through it! When we are being who and what we truly are, completely, we are moving ourselves back into alignment, so much so that the Magick of creation then reflects our spirit perfectly!

This is one of the chief reasons for ceremony. This is why we call upon the presence of spirits to help us. This is why we work with the elements of nature and proclaim the forces of creation to work with us!

THIS is how Magick is manifested!

Dare To BE! Dare To RISK! DARE TO SUCCEED!

To do or try, to play it safe or take a risk. There are in every instant of our lives so many choices we could be making, alternate paths we could be taking, leaving those set aside to the winds of time and character we just don't care to deal with, our paths are littered.

There isn't one of us who doesn't look back upon our lives at some point thinking how different life could have been had we made a different choice or had we set out upon another path. It's as natural to us as our very breath. We are much more than just movable chemistry after all.

We are living, soulful, spiritual beings with incredible and yes infinite perspectives into the possibilities that could be and can be, and that are! In part this is why we hold within our grasp such an expansive understanding not only of our own world and universe but also of the fabric of other dimensions and how we all do interrelate with each other.

Have you ever pondered on why it is that we can never seem to be satisfied existing in one mode of our own level of creation?

Why it is that we never stop trying to expand our understanding, to become more, to be better, to wax wiser, and to be more relevant in our lives and in our world?

It's at least in part because we know at our very core that we ARE more and that we have always been meant for more than we can possibly immediately grasp!

I remember helping a client once who was struggling his way through the early stages of recovery from trauma.

The issues he was passing through were complex and had haunted him for many years. . He was well aware that his behavior was an expression for seeking an altered state of mind that removed him from feeling all that he didn't want to feel and from facing the complexities of his own driving want to rise above himself and his past.

This gentleman was insightful, intelligent, and very much aware, so much in fact that I found myself needing to inject or intervene little at all with guiding words or insightful phrases. All that this soul really required was a willing ear and a sense of healing spirit through which to mirror what he had already answered for himself.

His own ponder resulted in the question to do or not, and, to be or not! This meaning of course, to allow himself to move on from his current dilemma or to continue residing in his self-ascribed stage of theater that he had set up for himself. In the end, he did choose to move on, simply because it was the best decision he could make for himself. Today that man is a very happy and successful businessman!

For him, he chose to take the risks and face the unknown of his future face to face!

We all face such living choices along virtually every corner of our path!

Many we shove aside. Many we choose to try and deny. Many we absorb and embrace!

But there are always those choices that we truly fear… and the fear itself can be debilitating to the shine of our sense of spirit!

These are the choices, the alternatives, the constructs of our being that we all have been afraid to face for all our own very personal and intimate reasons.

For all of us, to open wide that doorway to our own sense of fear-based revelation can sometimes seem like unleashing an unseen eternal struggle that we have been hiding within ourselves for all too long. Oh yes, much of it all is a rather benign perspective and not affective of our being remaining the thing of a particular personal character and little to nothing more.

Sometimes however, we harbor the unseen and incredible fears of our own successes and the rise to our own state of greatness, and for this reason there are sometimes very complex rivers of self-interpretation that we avoid and others we literally run away from!

It's all not that uncommon nor all that different than the struggles that other countless souls face in life where facing unknown and untested paths are concerned!

Can I do this?

Will I be alright?

How will I rise to the task?

How the hell will this all turn out?

Oh there are safe roads, smooth paths, the easy and safe ways through it all for sure!

Do what is safe!

Just take the tested paths where others have already proven it can be done!

What about our own sense of soul, of spirit, and our own need for meeting the vision of life within ourselves?

Do I have a mission in life?

It always comes back to that one Magickal question doesn't it?

WHY AM I HERE?

The real theme I'm striking for in this is to unfold the stopping gap where facing our own fears, of manifesting our own successes, of dealing with our own failures, and for believing in ourselves in our lives!

Yes, we can be motivated by others around us! We can get a sense of good feeling from reading the motivational phrases that other souls write and speak!

In the end however, all of that won't be there holding us up when the time arrives and we have to face ourselves and our own fears!

Will we make mistakes?

OH, PLENTY!

Will be recover from them?

Yes, every single one of them if we decide to do so!

Will we arrive at a point that we have envisioned in our minds? Perhaps not always in a crystal clear fashion, but the realm if sought, is in the end, MAGNIFICENT!

What is critical in all of this is to remember one single thing as you face such a point where you are beginning to set out upon your own path of impending successes in life!

To be is to not give up!

To risk is in the nature of accepting the truth of your own power and strength to rise upward and keep on rising!

To succeed is never a goal, but always an ongoing journey, for all of success is a living venture and never something we can just place on a shelf for the sake of our posterity!

BE! RISK! SUCCEED!

Then decide to keep on succeeding!

Darkness

Among those countless mysteries of creation that have resided throughout your human experience rests that eternal dichotomy sitting square between your interpretations of that which you perceive as Darkness and its grand inverse relationship to that of the Light, that shining presence that you see as residing at the core of your own soul!

When you close your eyes what you first perceive in this simple act through your senses is that of the Darkness that prevails itself over all other things right before your eyes. It's an enveloping quality that surveys of all things like a blanket of absence and cover, and perhaps it is from this instinctive reaction to your perceptions that you also tend to transpose your innate definitions of the dark throughout so much of your surrounding bits of creation?

Then of course there is the behavioral-set who rightly and justly draw attention to your instinct for self-preservation from the many beasts in your past and all that once threatened by hunting you down out of the dark!

When you seek to discover your answers to those deepest, most intimate, and unrevealed parts of yourselves, you don't liken this repository to the harbor of the light, you compare its storehouse to that of the Darkness within you all.

The Darkness has been used as a chief motivator for many things in your time here. It's been manipulated as a motivation for your fears, for control of your minds, for the mass bending of thought, and of articulating and altering the fabric of belief, and its manifestations have even been used to ensure your subservience as a people.

Darkness has been the prime example of all you are and should be afraid of in your world and of your fellows. It has been described as my dwelling place, and yet, the entire universe as you know it is comprised of its very essence in order to house the matter that makes possible your construct existence.

Yes, there are many forms of Darkness, what you think of it, what you project of it to be, and as it promotes in our minds. Then of course to what it all actually is! Darkness you see in at least a visual way to our cognitive and our mindful understanding is that quality of existence that simply is in relation to the quality of what is Light. They are two opposites of each other that cannot possibly exist without the other! Yet, you remain convinced that in order to survive and to gain a life after this one, or to simply remain safe in this experience you know as life, you need to fear the Darkness, while embracing the other, the Light!

It is a fascinating thing to consider over a nice cup of tea on a cold fireplace evening!

There in the Darkness, where you've always been afraid to look, of that deep well in your own understanding, where you thought you would discover all you've always been told was the worst to be feared in all of existence and in all of yourselves; there nested and preserved within the Darkness I submit; you will inevitably discover the footprints of those countless Angels that were placed there long before you even dared to imagine a subjective or an objective quality to all of that you see as the Darkness!

Destiny Despite Your Fear!

Eventually, inevitably, you reach a point where you find yourself standing in the presence of an emerging sense of self. Face to face with that which you become convinced has been constantly working, whittling against you in life.

That which you fear is a signal of your own absolute demise. Your spirit wants to give in, and your morale falters, friends desert you, and family stands in silent judgment of you and of what many might label ineptitude.

Then, is the time when you have the perfect moment of synergy, which awakens. Of mind, heart, spirit, and soul; then is when you gain a spark of illumination! It quietly and very calmly seeks to remind you that finally you have arrived at a point where your spirit is now aligning with that which has always, and will always be with you!

It reminds you that your strength is one with your soul, and your soul with the universe!

It reminds you….

Here, is where, destiny is born.

Destiny Due

Where destiny chooses it holds its due, manners subtle, fleeting, and throw,

into the wind, seems sordidly thin, in abundance of marvel we'd know.

Sweet mystery, such grace, veiled in its place, it traces its time and lieu,

breaded paths our way, embracing all our days, such seeking in where we'd go.

Now destiny's rind, is never so blind, it seeks our want and time,

emerge it will, when stepped by sill, when opened and welcomed in kind.

So embrace the Year, make paths run true,
time spells, and emergence will come,
the choice in time,
destiny's won fine wine,
revealing that Magickal tome!

How Long Will It Take to See If a Spell Worked?

I noticed this ponder posed by a good friend elsewhere today, but I chose my own website for the length and nature of my own thoughts on this marvelous matter of thought!

We can ask of this question: How long does or will it take for nature to reawaken a long sleeping forest? How long will it take for an inert and sleeping seed to grasp the energy of new life and break through its shell and raise up its neck from under the dirt into the warming sunshine?

How long has it taken Mother Earth to alter and shift her geological history to become the home that we now know?

Or, how long has it taken us to move from that first spark of our own sense of desire or want for life, and then, into those intents and motions of us forming the spell-work that instructs the forces of nature and of spirit to manifest all of that which we'll then be certain "WILL" emerge for us in our lives, if we truly expect anything to ever emerge at all for us!

After all, that latter part is indeed the grandest of all Spell-Making switches through and by which the rest of our Spell-Born intents do ever ignite and through which command creation to respond to!

One of history's brightest of minds in the art of witchcraft and spell-making who I admire, the Magi Israel Regardie, once said that it was his view that unequivocally he believed that the art of Magick was more than just a theorem to be postulated in an abstract way.

He contended that the path of Magick was a force of creation-making that could be proven both through empirical means and through the quality of experiencing its true manifestation in our own lives!

I can personally say that without any one single bit of doubt, I accept and support those words for I have experienced just this in my own life and have witnessed it in the lives of many of my personal friends!

Just how long does it take, or will it take, or "should" it take, for any certain "Spell" to work its art on the path of creation? Well, in my view that is a qualitative function tied to our beliefs more than any sort of a quantity to be measured.

Reaching back to the first whispers of my thoughts that I began with for a moment…,

When we all transition ourselves from our own wintertime season and onward into the new spring, we more than hope for or expect that nature will indeed awaken into a new blooming life. We without any one single bit of doubt, KNOW, that life "WILL" awaken and bloom into new colorful being!

This isn't a theory that we have formed in our minds! This isn't any sort of a question. We know that it is a certainty! We know that this will happen without ANY doubt!

Why?

Because this is the nature of all of the experiences we have watched and felt of the world around us throughout our entire lives! Just think on this for a moment! There is an incredible force of creative energy working throughout all of nature around us, in every microsecond, of every single moment, of every day, all working its energies to bring life alive!

Is this Magick at work in nature? YOU BET IT IS and we witness it from its inception into being!

As many have now come to both accept and believe, "spell work" and "spell-making" is no different! Even if its labeled as prayer to the God(s), or more complex articulations of the workings of the science of the spirit and of nature, for a spell to work, we must also without a question, hold a comprehensive belief that it "Will" work for us as we envision!

This is the nature of how and why spells do to work at all! we come to an elementary system and way of belief that what we intend, and work to spark into creation, while also working the science of our minds, our spirits, and through the science of nature, we draw our intents into manifested being! This is what spell work is and why it does what it does.

How long will or should we wait to see if our spell-work emerges into being for us before we back-step ourselves to work of it all over again?

How sure are you in what you intended and in what you believe?

How much of a certainty do you hold deep down in your soul that what you did or do will work to bring you into a state of your life where your spell comes into being for you?

The Gods brought creation together as it all has, and I might dare to state that any "timeline" probably wasn't on their minds in terms of when and if creation was to be formed in the grand schemes of all that is!

Creation and the universe "IS", because it was intended to be and that is it!

So instead of asking or seeking a timeline for how long it will or may take for your spell to work, or has it, or will it bring about an emergence at all in your life, perhaps another way of looking at it might help.

When you worked your spell, did you truly believe that it would bring a new way of being into your life? Or, did you question whether it would work at all, if it did at all?

If someone asks:

Do "SPELLS" and does spell-casting really work? How long does it or will it take to work?

Try responding to them as follows…

Do you believe in the ability of spell-making to alter the forces and the energies of creation to work in your favor?

If so, then it WILL work! It must! There is no maybe, or how, or when. It simply WILL and you must KNOW that it will.

As to when?

When and how long did you intend for it to work when you first cast your spell?

If you have read my thoughts on this, then you can see why I didn't present them in another forum! I'm too much of a big mouth!

Do No Harm but Take No Shit!

Some confuse the habit of a spirit of beneficent caring for self and others as also presenting yourself as some wimp to be walked over whenever it might please that bully that is always around some corner in life.

Sometimes it's the coworker. Sometimes it's that one neighbor you just can't get along with no matter how many smiles and how many apple pies you send over. Sometimes it's the soul who somehow crosses your path for no reason at all. Just because your living a life of good heartedness doesn't mean everybody is, and its these souls you would be wise in remaining at arms length between!

Remember, the wisest course in response to such confused people "IS" to simply turn and walk away, but when you can't, there is nothing in the beneficence books that says that you need to swallow sour peaches either! It's ok to stand your ground firm in your convictions! But remember to do so in such a way as to not compromise yourself also in the long run!

Live wisely and in forethought of your responses to irritants today and by irritants, I refer to those who would adore creeping under your skin like a rash! Stay centered in your resolve to yourself and to others today!

Do We Have God, Life, and Our Awareness All Wrong?

Good day everyone! There are days and times in life when our perspective appears progressively obscured, when those we thought friends suddenly seem to change their colors, when our outlook for all intents becomes misshapen, and the way of our path forward suddenly turns rather unsure. In such times let your spirits rise above it all and take in the balancing strength that is always there for us above the capacity of those many ill-toned rip-tides that will always be moving around us in one way or another.

We don't always have to have the answers as to why people, places, and things suddenly turn. What we can ALWAYS do is in response is to nest ourselves in those powers that creation has made available to us all! To reach for it, simply close your eyes and calmly think of such scenes as we know at our core personify a state of spirited power for you, and then allow yourselves to move towards it!

The key to the most powerful source of strength that we have at our avail has always been within us from the very beginning. The machinations of society and a long streaming period of culture and literal brainwashing with regard to the realities of those strengths and the real power that we all have within us have over the centuries whittled away at our own concepts of the awareness that unlocks and manifests these strengths.

Where Magick is concerned is but another way of describing this same pinnacle of power that many would rather we not hold any intimate adoration for. In their view, they would rather we all relegate such powers of creative strength and wonder to only those grander spiritual sources in creations spyglass.

Not discounting the actual meaning of these forces in all our lives, it remains in my view a grave cordon of injustice to deny of ourselves those same sources of creative power and strength that we have in the literal palm of our hands and at the core of our very existence!

Recently an article was released by Neale Donald Walsch relating to the ways that people are mistaken in how they connect their concepts of God and the ways that they paint this picture in their minds. Having read most of his writings on the subject, my immediate reaction to the spread in the booklet magazine was of course to generally agree with his opinions.

What quickly followed in my own train of thoughts however was that this was of course in the manner of our vast perceptions relating to life and how we unfold our entire living world in our minds! Is there a crystalized concept of God, of the Gods, or The Goddess that is more right than wrong, to be embraced and/or denied, for their lacking in a sense of their trueness to our souls?

We all hold diverse and separated threads of concepts of our own existence woven into our personal tapestries of spirit with regard to how we enchant our own spirits!

We not only engender and wax eloquent upon the chassis of our own foundations where our concepts of God, Gods, Goddess, and other valued creationist spirits are concerned. If nothing more, we all certainly do use these as launching points where are are formed the stepping stones upon which we make our way along day by day if time in and by itself is taken for what it truly is.

Time being but a perception of movement through the space of our dynamic spirits and not a measure of living linear action.

How we forge, create, and then choose to embrace those many forces that carry us through all of our good times and our not-so-good times are directly related to our own visions of the ways of God that we call our own!

Can we rise above the fray of our own discontents that arrive in daily life, of people, places, and of the things that never seem to meet our expectations?
Of course we can!
Its' all in the intent that we form and re-form in our lives again and again!

Does Hatred Have a Half-Life?

I'd rather tell you that hatred is devoid of any influence over the path, but if I did so, I'd be perpetrating an obvious lie. Yes, Magick is creation, it's belief in creation, steps on the path of creation, aligned with any and all beliefs, all ways of feeling, all ways of expressing, and this includes the harboring of those, the darkest of all of our inner-conceptions of our being.
In this, many tend to refer to it according to the color of its extremes. To most, it's known as; Hatred. Yes, it can be a powerfully influential force as we all are well aware. It can become an ideation against the construction of the progress of life in its worst forms, and in its extreme, it has brought humankind to the precipice more times than any other way we have ever known, and perhaps, will ever know.

In order to lay out where all of this is going, it might help to ponder the question; just what is Magick? In its most basic of understandings, let's simply say that Magick is the universal collective expression of the truth in existence to all of creation. An idea of creating, an ordered path with no limits, a construction of the emergence in any and all of reality no matter what path, or what particular order of belief that is followed.

The presence of vision and the mechanics of spirit and nature are all the same! To this then, an infinite amount of literature and belief has spanned our time here on our dear Mother Earth relating to this subject, so take all of this as you will in how you personally choose to believe.

Experientially, few would succeed in arguing against the precept that hatred can be a powerful force of creative emotion just like any other painted on the spectrum of our infinite repertoire of emergence! We all know too well what it's capable of creating and how its capable of manifesting around us.

Instinctively we all have an indicator within us that tells us that its capable of both bestowing and destroying quickly and efficiently, and it usually does so in the same manner with its breath as with its fists. Quicker in fact than most others if given enough elbow room to stretch itself out and to express its strength and opportunity.

Some say that hatred resides on the opposite side of love where creation is concerned. It's said that where love is bathed in warmth residing at the core of what we embrace as being best in our lives, of what is, the other, hatred, resides in the darkness on the other extreme end of that infinite prism of what our consciousness and emotion considers to be right, and good, and true if this can be applied at all.

It's said that emotion has both power and strength evocative and capable of manifesting the wildest and most extreme shifts on our path of life. It wouldn't be an ill formed conclusion then to say that as we feel, as humankind alters the face of its presence through its feelings and the emotions that we focus our spirits upon, then such would also be the propellant to states and in functions of practicing and manifesting any one or more infinite expressions of self-creation.

In other words, any of these being seen by those who practice and walk what we understand as the many paths in Magick just like any other form of spiritual or living ideal.

Just as free-will has been described and philosophically pondered in virtually every way since it was first conceived by man, we must also understand that there is no limitation upon the effects and or the veracity that one might just focus their creative potential upon when and if that soul feels a real sense of hatred for anyone or anything else to such an extreme level in their lives.

There are no end points to any way of feeling, to any emotions; but only the transition from one moment of feeling to the next until a sense of resolution has arrived. Magick is the same way. Just like prayers are to some forms of belief, as meditation resides in and affecting the soul, thus is Magick manifested and propelled throughout the world by the spark of creation.

In one way, you might say: "You say potato, I'll say po-ta-toe!"

The reality is that where the path of creation is concerned, emotion is a flashpoint, a primer, a source of ignition to anything we would or might imagine. Thoughtfulness and intent is another. I'm certain you get the theme now.

Can hatred be quelled? Does it truly contain a half-life and an eventual total death in our thoughts? Or would it be wiser for us to accept that on the logarithmic scale of feelings and emotions, that some form of anger and some form of hatred will always be with us as long as we are expressing the creative paths of life and being?

Then perhaps it might be wiser for us to depart this on the matter of ethics, and of human decency.

If not those fancy-suit-and-tie terms, then how about these on for size…

Perhaps the best bridge leading across the river of our hateful resentful discontent,...
Empathy and forgiveness?
These two have been known to extinguish some of the worst forms of hatred and anger along their way.

Durable Intent

The things that we seek in life are made manifest in our vision, powered by the alignment of our heart, and eternally housed in the core of our soul! It has the capacity to transcend any trial, surmount any opposition, and to bestow any blessing!
If life seems barren and without its touch, all we have yet to do is to merely unlock the vault of the mind in such a way so as to relinquish those reigns that are holding back the power of the spirit! In doing so, we turn the key that unlocks the infinite power of the soul, and of the universe!
Recently I read some thoughts of a very mindful soul in the path of emergence and his sentiments struck all too true. Right now there seems a present vast and a dark menacing tone that is being thrust into the public consciousness relating to witches and many followers of the "old ways" in so far as they are largely depicted as being aligned with the darker fortitudes of all things most-evil for the lacking in

any more of a graphic way of describing it.

Ah Hollywood!

In the days of World War 2 it was Roosevelt himself who dared to plead with filmmakers to produce works of film that would further the causes of war. It's how a personality like John Ford entered that fray. This is none other than mere truth.

You see, Roosevelt, as did the military and the then political establishment clearly recognized that what the public was exposed to on a continuing way both on the silver screen as well as in print, they also tended to lean towards as being more truth to real than other wise. Hence, the war and much of its impact was brought closer to the consciousness of the then civilized western world as were the causes of it all.

Can it be said that this was an attempt at a certain tuned manipulation of people's minds and a way to get people to lean towards certain directions where their feelings and their cooperation was concerned? Absolutely! Without a doubt as any social scientist would tell you! It was considered a sure necessity to the war effort. The Germans certainly thought so as did Hitler's then Minister of Propaganda Joseph Goebbels.

Now before anyone jumps there let me make clear that none of this is said in an attempt to liken to or to associate the efforts of the Allies to the warped ideologies of the German Propaganda machine of that day mind you. All it does is further exhibit what a continued exposure to the power of the media can do to both an individual's and to the public's conscious attitudes relating to the message at hand.

Now, back up to modern day.

In more common-era times there have been many attempts to regulate the messages relating to the true character of the older ways of spiritual thought to the world, with some successes shown for the efforts!

After all of the horror films have been produced and shown, after all of the sci-fi and fantasy has been wonderfully written, printed, and flashed across a projectionist's bulb, there is also a very real and a sound core to the valued ways of old, the ways of spiritual thought and adherence that has little to nothing to do with the anger, the hate, the darkness, the fantasy, and the evil that tends to make it to the celluloid universe, that being what it is.

The Witch, the Spiritualist, the Pagan realm as some try to name and define it, are all paths of a vast and a time-endless spirited wonder! Yes, also of mystery that existed long before many of the more modern schemes of religiosity were even sparks and droplets laid onto a page.

There have been marvelous and more objective screen writers and even religious representatives in the core modern churches of the world today who do admit and recognize that just because a body of souls choose to follow one of the "old ways" doesn't in any way mean that such ways should be considered woven into the fabric of any sort of evil.

The ways of the Witch are the age-old ways of the science of nature and of the ultimate spirit!

The ways of the followers of the old-religion walk the paths of inner consciousness, of creation's wonder, and they meld and blend their philosophies of life and spirit within and throughout the context of what are yet again, by some, being painted and depicted as being archaic, evil, and against the more modernly acceptable philosophies of spiritual goodness and truth.

Nothing could be further from reality!

Most practitioners and followers of the old ways, do so in peaceful soulful unions with one another. Most seek peaceful collective conscious cooperation with all others, as with the ways of all of nature around them. Most seek the illumination of the mind, heart, soul, and the spirit.

Most seek enlightenment of thought and to open wide the gateways that conduct the falsehoods that oppose a true sense of peace and path.

The next time you watch a movie or read an editorial view on the dark and evil ways of the Witch, or of some other path written throughout the landscape of the old world, remember to also draw forth the truths relating to what has been wrought of those forms of belief that have conducted abuses and even brought about the darkness and the deaths of so many others in the world today, and yesterday.

Hollywood is wonderful! Although, not always purveyors of the way things REALLY are or really could be!

Emergence!

Do You Think You Have the Power to Change the Entire World?

I was recently moved by the inspiring thought that regarding our path and our purpose for being here, it all really boils down to this. In the grandest of visions which is the vision that each of us holds within, in each of our ways, in all of the inseparable elements of our soul, we come here unfolding a chart, or yes, a book of our life if you will.

Nothing is ever set in stone or a pretext to necessarily "be" beyond our own power or the capacity to affect the emergence of our soul. We are the ultimate expression of what "will be" according to why we came and to all we learn to be along our way. We emerge from a state of wonder and into a dawning state of "I AM" instead of wandering aimlessly seeking spotlights to guide us along with only a guess as to where we are all going. Its part and parcel to why the elders among us all eventually say things such as:

"If I knew then what I know now," and "Why is it that youth should be wasted on only the young?" Eventually there is an elemental spirited switch that goes off somewhere on the path of our life, a "spiritual connector" if you will that simply makes itself known to us where we instinctively come to the resolve within that we are more than simply ourselves on an all alone trip.

We come to the resolve that in all of this, the "I" has now suddenly been joined with, not replaced by mind you, but joined along with a "WE" experience. Our charts are individualized by and for us, to live and to experience and to embrace. But collectively, they are an expression of "WE".

"I AM" is the result of our being and our becoming all that we would be. "We ARE", is the result of ascending from who we were, feeling all alone, and into who "I NOW AM". A fantastic and a wonderful trip it is for each of us!

Since our very first breath to the lasting glimpse of our shining eye, our presence carries light all along our way!

We came into this world changing everything due to our sudden presence! In our first years here we altered the lives of all of our family permanently and then influenced and altered the world around us as our years progressed.

As we lived and as we expressed our power upon the fabric of existence, we changed everything and everyone we touched in our own way! Had we never come into this life in the first place, and the entire world that became ours would have been a drastically different place, but that's not what happened!

What DID happen is that we DID come, and yes, due to our being here, we DID CHANGE OUR ENTIRE WORLD, one little bit, one mere place, one solitary soul, one shifted effect at a time throughout all of our years here!

If we project our "presence effect" in terms of raw numbers,...... CAWING CROW!!!

Over the years and expanding upon the ripples of people, places, and countless things that were touched and thus altered by our influence can run into the thousands and tens of thousands in terms of people, places, and the perspective of dimension only knows how many things!

Think about that for just a moment and you begin to dawn to the truth.... WOW!!!

Now there's REAL POWER in the ability for one spirit to change an entire world!

Energy

Energy is at the source of all things! Your intent embraces it, your thoughts and emotions amplify it, and your action increases its dynamic! This is the way of CREATION!

Essential Parts of Magick

The essential fabric of Magick is as simple or as complex as one might wish to make of it in the mind. In truth the simplest essential factors necessary to direct the fabric of Magick are:

Spirit – whereby the willful source and spiritual strength proposing and supporting the intent of the action,

Device or Instrument – any tool, material which is the object of the focus of will, and,

Incantation – in thought and more commonly by citation the action of some desired outcome.

Feeling Real Magick!

We may fall, we may stumble, we might vary our path for a bit, and yes, we might simply make ill choices requiring correction and no doubt more.

Nothing however, ABSOLUTELY NOTHING in life should ever be allowed to convince you to cower or lower your head in any way, to think of yourself as lesser than, or that you are anything but the Magnificence that YOU ARE!

You want to see and feel real Magick working in your life?

Then UP STAND TALL!

Face others UP CLOSE AND EYE TO EYE and then, IGNITE THE MOST POWERFUL PART OF YOUR SPIRIT AND LET FLY YOUR MAGICK RIGHT TO THE STARS AND BEYOND!

Do this, and trust me,…. you ain't seen nothing yet!

Finally Embracing Your Path in Life!

After having lived through enough trial and pain in your life, having falling to ashes and then later rising from it like the Phoenix; once you have chosen to become truly acquainted enough with yourself, gotten used to the idea of your own value and then begun to embrace your own shining talents that can serve others and the world;

once you have finally started to grow into your own and chosen to set out onto your new and emerging path which grievously might also include departing from the accompaniment of some of those whom you once thought would never leave your sphere; then, and only then, will you understand what it is to embrace your true path in this life and to foster all of that you are truly capable of!

After which, let your shining light continue to emerge until it drowns out self-doubt, personal obstruction, and all that would serve to darken your path, and then, make the greatest magnificence of your path for the benefit of others and thereby of course, for yourself!

You see, as there are certainly some who come into this world seeming to be naturally "connected" to their as yet unfolded destinies in rather obscure and yet determinist fashions, there are so many others among the rest of us who travel the path of experiential-determination.

In simpler terms, we stroll and stumble our ways along until we either smack ourselves silly enough times or we end up doing things and taking actions that somehow lead to us dropping flat down onto our faces which in many ways serve as the very ashes of our own demise from a state of being where we thought we belonged.

From this now demolished state we rise up again and begin to move around aimlessly until we make some sense out of all that had happened? This which for those destined to such paths, evolves incredibly into an absolute revelation of the soul and of the spirit! In other words, we are suddenly inspired and thus onward we FINALLY GO!

Yes, in typical fashion these are admittedly exhibitions of the two widest end points on the spectrum of life experience to the paths of life, but through this you get the idea!

In between under that incredibly complex bell-curve are all of us with our own destinies, our own tastes, our own drives, our own commitments, and our own adopted responsibilities. Somehow within and woven into all of these infinitely laid out tapestries in creation, every single one of us resides with our own individual life!

Odd that the old analogy of the grain of sand on a beach should appear in thought at this juncture eh? Yes, the more that I exist here and the more that I find myself working with people, walking the path as a helper, a healer, a seer, a paranormal detective, a motivational and seminar speaker, and an intuitive or a psychic medium if you will, the more convinced that I am that we can imagine ourselves as grains on that very beach of existence!

Nothing regretted and everything to gain, we all find our own paths and our own reasons for either reaching outside of ourselves for greater and more imaginative inspirations or we withdraw into the schism of belief that says that there is nothing else but "we", and we are really absolute nothingness that chaos concluded should exist for the sake of absolute nothingness!

You as we all carry our own torches and our crosses if you will and we paint our own personal definitions onto and into our lives! From this, eventually, we clean the dust and the path dirt off of our robes and we find ourselves at the point of a blatant and an unremitting acceptance of all we have been told we are, or, we turn away from such outdated and outmoded paradigms of the poor precision of a diminished sense of spirit and choose to believe that:

We are more!

I AM MORE!

We were meant for more!

We stop believing those ludicrous social definitions of being that seem to serve only a minute few and leaves the masses to the degradation of weathering, unfortunate states of negation, and plain and simple outcast diminishment.

We will seek out the answers to our being and set them to the music of creation!

To believe in any way that you, I, or that any of us are anything but brilliance and genius in form, is to set a vision of existence as simply mundane and meaningless!

There is more to why you and I are here and eventually if you silence the spirit and soulful numbing noise protruding from the world around you for just a little bit, and if you seek yourself deep within and all that you truly are and were meant for, eventually you will find your way!

Then, the stars and the sky itself can never stop you!

Never stop asking "why?"

Fulcrums in Revelation!

There are souls who for some great undiscernible reason find themselves standing upon pivot points of alteration, fulcrums on the latitude of creation, standing upon never ceasing landscapes of periodic lazy-Susan's that insist upon change regardless of desire, want, or necessity.

It's not without respite that I can appreciate such feelings. Honestly, I've spent the better part of my life feeling as if I were teetering upon such fulcrums without any real understanding as to why? It can grow to be quite a frustrating place to be in time.

Being always manipulated, skewed, carried along parabolic adventures with only a vague, if veiled comfort in knowing that there always was, or would yet surely be some reason for it all.

Let me ask you… Have you ever crossed the path of someone, landed in some place, or found yourself faced with some situation, that would in time dawn to be incredibly important to the unfolding of your way forward in your life?

Have you ever known a time of great trial, incredible challenge, a period of real suffering that in time led you to a rise to a much higher, to a greater awareness of yourself that no doubt probably would have not dawned without such trial?

Fulcrums are funny things aren't they? They are points, centers of change whereby creation centers its forces, and the rest of things seem to sway about them turning everything else altered unbeknownst. They are points of force, centers of magic that are focused outward and inward.

They may even be called the purveyors of the nexus of creation to great change!

You, I, we, those of us who deep down have gone through incredible periods of life always asking the same question; yearning of creation, for the Gods themselves to give us some qualified answers as to why? Why here? Why me? Why now? What did I do to deserve all this?

In truth, we know. We all know.

Many just haven't allowed for the flame of that level of awareness to be illuminated yet!

Open the gateway, because…

It's time good soul! Your time is now!

If this strikes you, I mean REALLY strikes a chord within you for some reason. Then there is a reason and you know it!

How's that for revelation?

The Devil's Grimoire of Our Destiny

The book of your chart is a foretold Grimoire, an eternal flower to be sure! Its pages are neat and it's tender so fleet, as our path that we set out endured. Before our days here were even in play, our outline we laid down and absorbed so wise, for our purpose in this was our presence called bliss, yet conceived in nary, perfect, surmise. Then we set ourselves out to live it, sufficient! This was to be what we yet again would know as the path of our life!

We do as you see refer back to its pages and its pleas as we wander our way on back across the veil in regular forays! Its pages realign, induce power supine, all in wait of our marvelous enduring gait!

Trust yourself and your intuitions where your path is concerned!

Nobody knows better or is more sure why it is and for what purpose you came here! If we would only remember that part of the theater hand-bill of life when we are amidst our so many difficulties! Then we would be innately better in allowing ourselves to navigate our way back to remembering this universal truth!

Never is there a perfect formula to be applied to any stretch of our path. None of it was ever intended to unfold as perfect! The perfection as much as it ever would be is all wrapped up in how we allow our own vision to become our own reality!

How much personal power and how much of the personal vision of your own being are you willing to invest and apply to the path of your life? Try asking, is there something I'm avoiding about myself that could be affecting the emergence of everything that I KNOW I am capable of and am destined to become? What is it about my own fears that is veiling and covering over my own brilliance? What am I not facing about myself that is stalling this power and this strength from blooming? And perhaps the better way of putting it all: What am I willing to risk of myself in order to make good upon my own path?

Every question, every aspect, every bend, and twist, and turn, have all been foreseen and foretold in the pages of your own chart, the Grimoire you wrote of yourself, from the core of yourself. As are all of your strengths and the very core of the nature of the inner-power that makes you, YOU, as NO OTHER!

The Path, Your Path!

Many have wondered that if our lives have been laid out in such an advance fashion, why is it that so much seems to go so wrong for so many along their way?

To this there is only one truth that can and does encompass every possible construct. It's an old rule, as old as our consciousness, and yes, even long before that. It's usually referred to as "free will", or destiny, and/or the path of self-determination.

The Devil you see is not in the pudding as it were, it's always been right in your soul! How you choose to invest yourself to the purpose of your path, according to who you are, is entirely your own affair! How you define it, realize it, work at it, laud of it, and wax eloquent upon it is your choice!

Nothing in all of creation will ever force you to BE anyone or anything you choose to not be!

I suppose that as we all ponder on the many twists and turns that we will encounter along our way, a better and clearer question may be:

Now ask yourself…

Do you believe in your own Magick? If so, why? If not, why not?

Do you believe in spirits, the force of the Devil, and in spirits from within you? If so, why? If not, why not?

Do you believe in the capacities you harbor within yourself?

If so, perhaps then that's all of the Magick and power that is necessary for you at the moment!

For some people, POWER isn't so much a word or a term to be feared because of old ways of thought. For them it's not illusion and nor the thing of legend domain.

For some people, the power in their lives disappeared so very long ago.

All that was left for them, was a cold and hard life to now be faced.

Life somehow lost its imagination! It lost its power! It lost its….. Magick!

One of the greatest of all secrets to any bit of real power that we allow to become new beginnings, is that we make our imagination real for ourselves! We BELIEVE IN OURSELVES AT LAST! This is real inner-power! This is real inner-strength!

We touch the fabric of nature! We allow ourselves to totally and completely open wide the gateway to our own spirit and then allow the universe to applaud us to our efforts!

This is the real Magick to be accepted that leads to it all, direct from the core of ourselves!

Believe in your imagination, for this is where true power comes!

How Do People Use Magick?

If you would know……People have asked, "what is the most powerful source of magick?" To this I usually respond that to those who have and are purveyors of Magick, lifelong students of the way of the path, there is but only one ultimate source of all the energy that's contained in Magick!

We are but a source of transmutation, we are living crystals, we're focal points that interpret, relate, and that channel! But if you don't first spend time building an intimate relationship with yourself by truly becoming your own best friend, then it might as well be so that you intend to continue working as your own worst enemy!

In Belief…. Magick Begins….

Sometimes you just have to trust that the stars will continue to shine upon you!

Among the many sources and writers that I've referenced over the years in the subjects of Magick, of the spirit, and of the path, there are several certain knowledgeable souls who I've concluded did seem to have a much firmer grasp than did others on those greater truths empowering the path!

These souls all in their own ways promoted the idea that we, in and being those who continue to seek out the path of the awakening in the root-works of our own Magickal strengths; can and always will remain virtually absent in some clarity in the force of our own inner-powers without also sweeping away the dust that obscures the accompanying clear and sure understanding of what and how we think and feel about ourselves firsthand!

That we would inevitably find it a missing critical figure in the formula of our own construct of being does seem to boggle the minds of those who would conclude that such a brilliance as Magick in the world, is but only a fictional way of thought when they would also choose to align their own thinking to that of the brilliance that resides in the answers of their prayers for themselves.

It doesn't really matter though, for as we all embrace and engage our own living sense of spirit with regard to our own ways of believing, we also add to that collective power and strength of the human spirit of the world! Even when we don't consciously choose to do so. It's all in how creation works actually!

As we walk our paths, one by one, day by day, bearing our own witness to the wonders and to the fearful that is our current world, it's also an easy thing to begin to feel a bit lost amidst a sea of lacking firmness of our own particular surety!

This is when I always try to recall a triumphant statement I once heard cried out by a certain grand statement that I admire!

"WE ARE ALL STARS!"

True enough!

Even to the point of both learning and accepting that we are all INDEED all made up of the fabric of all of that "STAR STUFF" as Carl Sagan used to point out!

The further grand creative universal truth that I try to put out there ahead of me on each morning of every day, and especially so when I am feeling especially fearful for some reason for my own path, which of course I do at times as everyone does!

This truth is that we ARE the stuff of the stars! It exemplifies what I AM! What we all are! It exemplifies just from where ALL forms of Magick begin, and end! Even that Magick held within the many forms of prayer that are expressed throughout the world!

This truth is embraced and manifested in that:

"IN BELIEF.... MAGICK BEGINS...."

It's also from where it stops, stalls, is held back, and from where on many levels it is denied!

BUT…

It can never be eliminated!

Why?

It's simple really…. You see, "Magick" is what many call that stuff from where creation itself was born!

Try negating creation!

Yes, "WE ARE ALL STARS", and no matter how fearful you, I, or any of us may feel about our lives on any given moment, or any given day, it will always remain true….

"IN BELIEF…. MAGICK BEGINS…"

In The Spirit of Excalibur!

The spirit of Excalibur is more than just a tale, it's an ICON in our vast culture that exhibits that force of spirit that resides within us all!

All that we need do in order to uncover and realize our own true potential is to stop, breathe, and to straighten our backs and then take a stand in our lives!

Dare to BE YOU!

Make manifest that Magick that sparks from your soul! DARE TO BE POWERFUL NOW IN YOUR LIFE!

On the Devil's Path, Honor Above All Else!
The path of illumination!
Honora Super Omnes!
"Honor Above All Else"
The person who strives to live within this code of conduct lives within a code of the spirit! We all know right-well that it's not a simple statement of fashion, or a trend.

We know that it's a manner in how we choose to treat others and in how we express ourselves to the world around us that serves to align us along a position of revealing the true path that is always in wait for us!

I was recently reminded of the importance of this by a certain shining soul who blesses my circle. The critical importance that this commitment to a state of character and all that it influences, upon everything relating to our soul, our strength, our power!

Interestingly enough, when I personally began to delve into the ancient arts of the craft I was about 13 or so in years. By that time in my life I had already bathed my mind into research on my family heritage, from where we came, from what we considered our lineage, our past, and what their practices and beliefs were.

I remember being so incredibly interested in the power that their manners of belief had upon their lives so long ago. In subsequent years I would come to deeply understand that as it was so revered back in the days of the ancients, the same must be true for those of we in the craft today!

How we align ourselves with our true intents, with our beliefs, in how we choose to treat others, our fellows, our "kin" if you will; how we honor our associations, and in how we present ourselves and live within the rubric of our actions all have a profound effect upon the life of our path and upon the power and the strength of our Magick. It has the capacity to either build us up and/or to tear us asunder.

Thus is the nature of the force of our spirit through which we ultimately find ourselves judged, by our intents, and through our actions, more than could we ever by any one other soul.

You see, thus far in my life throughout the arts of Magick and of spirit and strength, I've found that there is but one great and albeit insurmountable force that has the capacity to both build us up to the heights of infinity, as well as to tear us down to literal ashes.

It resides in our absolute and free choice to live and to practice our arts in a spirit of honor above all else. Want, greed, lust, need, healing, revenge, to help, or to avenge, it all fetters down to one ultimate quality that tunes and tones the path of our Magick and the tone of our ultimate sense of spirit.

It is all contained in our actions of walking the path in the craft with either a sense of honor, or not to do so.

When we choose to turn ourselves away from this sense of honor, of a loyalty to our "kin", to ourselves in the arts, to the living spirit of our ancestors, we serve to misalign ourselves from the true source of all the power and strength that might otherwise serve to build us up beyond the peaks of infinity!

When we choose however to live and act within the spirit of honoring our ancestors, and especially to honor ALL of those we have chosen a commitment to serve in some way, for the better good will of all their paths in life, we reach out for and gain everything we could ever hope for in the way of true power, strength, and of Magickal brilliance!

The choice is simple.

The results, obvious, sometimes all too obvious.

The sad thing is, it's not always given but a glimpse.

The saddest thing is, when its all thrown to the wind.

INTENT- The Ultimate Dream Maker!

Within us all is a set of spirited gear-works all working together like some fantastic machination wrought of creation itself!

Think of it as one single extension of an arm of the universe swinging and manifesting everything seen, felt, and heard, and of all that was, all that is, and all yet to be! It's rather ironic really when you stop to think about it. How often have you spent a considerable amount of time thinking of some want for your life, some "dream" that you thought you would give anything to experience! Then all of a sudden, somehow, and in some mystical and magickal way, it emerges into your life!

What is it that brought it all about some ask themselves?

Hard work? Oh surely! The result of a blessing? Oh MOST assuredly! The instance of what an old friend of mine used to call "plain and simple crap-luck?" NEVER!

There is no such thing as luck. You see, every elementary cog, wire, and spirited spark that makes up that infinite engine of creation is all fueled by one thing and one thing alone!

INTENT

It's the quality of our individual and our collective intent that creates all that we are. It's the power and the ultimate strength that is fueled by our individual and our collective intent that both manifests new experience and it shifts and changes existing paths of being!

World events are skewed and affected by it just as every single instant out of the lives of every soul are crafted and adapted out of the affectations of our intents.

The truth is that from Plato and Socrates to the realm of the Gods themselves, from the quality of your favorite verse that speaks of the creation of the universe, our world, and of life, to the sparkle of a new born baby's glimmering eye, every single moment that we call our own is something we create for ourselves!

The same can be said for the power that is behind everything that we emerge in our lives, even when things don't work the way that we would wish.

When it is that matters and situations don't seem to be working in our favor, first try to ponder on how much energy you are giving to those instances of thought where you visualize and imagine them NOT working out rather than providing ALL, every single bit of your thoughts and your energy into focusing your intent on making them become real, regardless of all and anything to the contrary!

This is part of why successful souls speak so ardently regarding never listening to those opinions that would have you beginning to believe that you cannot do or become something or someone you know right well you ARE and all you know you can BECOME!

It is in the purity of INTENT whereby we center and manifest the POWER and the PURITY of our energy into making it BE-COME real in our lives!

This is where the term "BE-COME" originated from!

We cause the experience of life to "COME" onto our path, then it shifts from a state of "coming" and into a state of "being."

Intent IS INDEED that ultimate dream maker for if it wasn't for the power of intent to create reality, nothing would exist in the first place!

WE ALL ARE INTENT MANIFESTED! It is through such intent that we thus manifest!

Intuition and Understanding

The masses reside. The countless abide. The seekers review. The followers imbue. The makers succeed. The few sow seed. But it's the individuals that intu', who are the ones to break through to those deeper mysteries in creation and of the Gods! Its such souls who open wide the gateways whereby the grander aspects of creation are set forth revealing the remainder of all that is to those minds daring to understand.

Is There Magick on the Yellow Brick Road to Gay Marriage?

I find myself writing this particular BLOG entry wondering what it is that's motivating me to begin this text and I keep returning to those several postings from people I know personally on social networks that simply befuddled my mind.

I never knew they had harbored so much intense hatred towards others in such ways, and then realized that as I read, these souls obviously had no idea that I was indeed one such of the same souls who they were intentionally chastising with their level of damnation.I found myself admitting, yet again, that I've grown so tired and weary of hatred and divisiveness between people and communities, not only between souls and people in the Pagan and Witchcraft community, and between the larger Religious Belief communities, but with regard to my own intimate life as well.

You see,....when the ruling came down regarding gay marriage from the United States Supreme Court I kept thinking to myself that I was not going to say much if anything at all. Not because I didn't have my own personal reasons for being pleased about it all. I am most!

It certainly had nothing to do with the fact that I really wanted to stay removed from any of it in any public way. Nor did my feelings on the matter have anything to do with the fact that I harbored any ill of will relating to it all, for I surely didn't and don't. I can't really!

This especially given the fact that I am and have been Gay my entire life and have out of the closet for well over a decade!

I simply wanted to revel in a reserved and in a very personal way about it all.

Why? Well, to put it plainly, I used to be one of those souls serving others in the trenches of activism for a good number of many years, and in my mind, I just enjoyed watching so many others celebrate and stand "up and out" in and amidst a world that is slowly and in the swings of its own struggles, awakening to the greater truth of humanity's path!

For many years now I've stepped back into the shadows where I've discovered my own brand of thoughtfulness is a bit easier to let run free.

For many years I trudged in the trenches of social work, and I mean this quite literally mind you! I worked in those social community areas that many labelled as "ground-zero social work!" I counseled and supported IV drug, other drug users, and alcoholics, helping them to seek out and enter treatment.

I worked with and helped the HIV and AIDS community for many years. I was an activist in the Massachusetts needle exchange debates of their day. There was even an expansive period when I served on Boards for the Disabled community! In my past throughout it all I even found myself testifying before Joint Sessions of the Massachusetts State House and Senate where Bill passage was sought to help persons with disabilities including those persons suffering from HIV and AIDS and those struggling with substance abuse.

I've worked in high profile capacities with Public Health Departments in these capacities. I had become used to having my face and voice being out there and had just decided that the time for me had passed. Done.

At the end of the day, I simply considered my time in all of this light paid and served, and just figured that I had made the decision a long time ago to leave all of this to those who now wanted to be down there walking that path.

None of my feelings however mean that I am not elated over this ruling, because of course I AM! How could I not be after all?

Finally, after a long and treacherous road, American freedom had once again rung its great bells for all of the world to hear and yes, I am proud of the day and I am so happy for the many who find themselves just a little bit less restricted today as a result!

In no way am I deluding myself thinking it's all over mind you! As with other such struggles in our past, there will be a long and as treacherous upward road to be travelled for us all. We will see and experience days and times when certain souls will choose to express themselves in darker and segregated ways relating to all of this.

There will be religious fanatics who will make it their mission to serve the cup of degradation and hell and damnation that in their view will send so many others to face perditions flames because of their thoughts on those words "Love" and "Marriage."

At the time of my exit from all of this age of my own activism, I decided that I couldn't deny it any longer to myself, I had burned out big time from it, and just when I was in the midst of my own personal "coming-out!" Talk about a blessing and a nightmare all at the same time! Nothing could have been better and worse for me at that time, and it was, but all of that's another long story that I won't bore you all with. It could be the basis for a novel in and by itself, BELIEVE ME!

The bottom line for me is simple…

There is a blessed Magick to the path of life that can only be wrought by our soul, and if there is one thing that's for certain,…

Where there is the expression of Love in any form, then there is also the expression of the best brand of Magick that any little bit of creation could ever shine in our world!

I find myself praying for peace and asking for a little bit of the Magick that is LOVE to work where little else seems able.

Just Who and What is it that Will Change Everything?

Eventually, after enough sweat, after enough struggle and enough worry, you realize that you just have to have faith in your intuition and know that when the High Priestess is drawn and when the Ace of Cups accompanies her, the common theme shining between the two is a storm of the thunder and lightning of creation that has just been waiting to be illuminated!

If there is one thing more than anything else that serves to disperse our sense of a heightened awareness of ourselves, it is that skewed bit of obscurity in our own vision that we would insist upon continuing to place before our own thoughts and beliefs.

The old theme recants, that in so many ways we can always be both our best friend and our worst enemy at the same time! Doubts in decision making. Doubting in our trouble-shooting capacity for life's problems. The continuing presence of so many obstructions and recurring problems that regardless of the spirited propellant that drives us forward, we keep on trying to convince ourselves that somewhere, somehow, sometime, there is a proverbial "sabo" waiting to upset our path all over again!

In truth, in time, if we finally get out of our own way for a while, we may just come to understand that this is NOT the truth at all! This is the revelation that awaits us all!

This is that paradigm shifting truth that will finally begin to change everything for us!

Within us all you see is a key, a golden key that opens the gateway to an unspeakable and endless river of intuition and awareness! When we realize that accompanying this level of heightened and unstoppable awareness is a power of spirited creation beyond compare, as with the Ace of Cups, what it is really trying to depict for us is the inspiration that we all harbor within a strength of vision and a power of Magickal creation for the fabric of reality and dimension that can and will change anything…. Yes, ANY-THING!

The greatest religious and spiritual masters throughout history knew this and a few actually lived it. These are the souls who are always thought of as having risen above everyone else!

These are the souls who broke with tradition and who broke new ground shifting paradigms of thought and belief in such paramount ways that the thunder of their consciousness shifted reality itself!

They are the ones who will always mark the patterns of history and who are never forgotten for their individual influence upon civilization!

One of the most difficult things to come to grips with is that each one of us has this same capacity within ourselves to change our path and to alter the very fabric of our own reality in such ways so as to alter the very fabric of dimension right along with it!

What it all boils down to is belief!

Belief in yourself! Belief in your intents to emerge into being! Belief, true and unwavering firm belief in the power that you hold at your core to see, to do, to create, to alter, and most of all, TO BE!

THIS is what changed the lives of those masters and this is what altered EVERYTHING!

Oh, and this is what continues to alter everything!

The question is, will you believe it and believe in yourself enough to transcend the veil of dimension and of reality?

To Be a Healer

To be a healer, is being a helper, a teacher, a seeker of knowledge, a giver, a warrior, a protector, a seer, a guide. If this is your path, may you walk it with honor, light, and integrity! – Author unknown

A gracious good morning and a fine dandy of a day to you all my dearest friends! Magick is in the heart! The Devil's Path is in the soul! Magick walks along with us, right through our days of olde!

Ultimate Spirit!

I think it may be time to re-cap a thought for some out there with regard to just what is meant when those such as myself use the term "Magick?"

What is being referred to in its many general forms isn't the "Magic" with a "c" being that showman flair of stage illusion; but the "Magick" with a "k" that is some path of an ancient way of believing that conjoins the studies into the science of nature, with that of the spiritual path of a way of believing!

It's not all that uncommon to most other forms of belief of the world, wherein as we all engage in some form of prayer, some way of spiritual alignments, practice observances, and embrace of our own ways of believing in the purity of our own soul and spirit in its connections to the vastness of that we see as creation, there are those who also make it their living path to study the connections of the spirit to that of the manifestations of the creative forces of all of nature that surrounds us!

In my personal life I recently yet again found myself in the position of providing a generalized watered-down explanation as to the outward appearances of our way of believing to the soul who on looking in must stand in some amazement at just what all of this must be about.

Congruence!

You will always fail to realize the full 100% of your own essence through continually trying to be some-thing you are not, and/or in trying constantly to convince yourself that you are not some-thing that you know right-well that you are!

Most make a lifestyle out of walking through their days persistently out-of-synch with their own true selves, throwing their essence into an "out-of-the-loop" division of itself! In such a state, nothing can ever totally be as it was meant to be! When you finally realize and move yourself towards your own congruent state of truth, and you bring into balance what has for so long "resided completely divided" on the outside fringes of your true essence, you become a prism of POWER that cannot ever be undone again!

A great part of what we do when we cross the veil as we are at rest is to remind and to help us to constantly realign ourselves to our true selves again!

Have a calm, a peaceful, and an illuminating night!

What is the Devil's Path many ask?

It is the path of ultimate and unrestrained illumination!

This only arrives after one has gained real and true congruence!

Alignment

Well, if anyone ever wished to seek any understanding of that alignment which feeds mine own, try then seeking out the vestiges of that man who was known as Churchill. I need not say any more of myself.

Is there any such a thing as an alignment of the spirit, that has the potential to both feed the power of our spirit through us as well as potentially working against it?

None of us ever seem to act within any sort of what we might honestly refer to as "perfection", yet every bit of that which works both within us, and through us, is an absolute expression of the ultimate perfection of creation! Its why Magick works! We know this!

Its why we continue to seek out continued knowledge and understanding, advancement and superiority, a greater expanse of our collective presence and our own greater advancement!

We know, deep down somewhere within ourselves that we ARE greater, that we ARE more powerful, and that somewhere within us are the keys that will unlock the power of eternity up to us. It's why we as sentient beings, NEVER stop! We know that we ARE Magick! In some way.

I've heard it said time and again that Magick, as with many things, is a double-edged sword. It can work with us. It can work against us. We can open ourselves up to its manifest power and strength, or we can shut ourselves off of it and turn ourselves away from its very presence. It's always a choice and a path to be aligned or skewed.

Yes, aligned!

The image of the sword really is an image of power and of an ultimate alignment with that of nature and creation for a good reason. It is a symbol and a tool that crafts and articulates direction! It focuses our intent, and it sharpens the force of our spirit to the creative forces of nature in construct and conjoint ways. The symbolism of the wand does exactly the same thing.

Although, the sword and its shining blade does make for a more exhibitive example of the force of our spirit working the forces of nature to, for, and/or against the "nature" of our spirits!

In ceremony we open and close circles, we draw forth our minds into centers of themselves, and yet also seek to expand the conscious force of our thoughts, our minds, and our spirits making of them creative extensions of our souls asking of nature and creation to work for us, with us, and not against us!

Though as we all know, there are times when indeed, it seems the forces of nature, creation, of spirit, and of Magick do seem to work so against us when we obviously wish otherwise! In such times, perhaps seek out the basis of your thoughts, your greater levels of thinking, and the actions that your thoughts may be having upon the

Magick that you are or have been seeking to shift, alter, or create along your path and in your life!

Think on this for a moment if you will. If we espouse and act in one way in our lives, asking people and the world to see of us and to accept us in certain ways, and we then think and covertly act in yet entirely other aligned ways of being, in the end we will be working against ourselves point blank and done. The forces of the universe, of creation, of Magick and of spirit will not only be miss-aligned; it could be said that they would remain warped. Interesting that there are those who might say of someone else, that this other soul just doesn't seem right, as if something about them just isn't quite as it seems.

We can work with or against ourselves usually in quite innocent a fashion without even realizing it consciously. Then again, we all know that there are those who do it, quite consciously. There are many ways of coping, or conducting ourselves throughout varied places, settings, groups, and environments all of which carry their own respective strains and concerns.

In the end however, how we think, accords with how we act, and how we act, universally sets an alignment that is an expression of our intent that is one of the greatest of keys to the gateways of all of our Magickal concerns.

In the simplest of ways of looking at it, it really is not a confusing archetype.

If we show up for life in our truest guise as we honestly are and then seek an alignment of both our understanding of the way that we are thinking and acting, then to seek out to express these ways in the Magick we seek to create, well, the rest really does fall into its own, "alignment" doesn't it?

Mysteries Veiled

Mysteries hide veiled in plain sight rising like roses in the sun, and when we earn the right to learn our destinies will then be one. For nothing endeared is ever feared thus knowledge is our key, unlock its sage brought into this age, then thus we'll finally see.

The Mystery of Why?

Why is it that pain seems the greater constant in life, while happiness and joy seem so momentary and fleeting a thing...?

Why is it that there are those who believe they have the right to take the lives of others,...?

Why is it that if you think or believe, or even look differently from someone else, that this automatically puts you in the position of being lesser or some sort of enemy...?

Why is it that understanding always seems to be so far off from our reach, and misunderstanding always standing so close by our side…?

Why is it that there are so many mysteries that seem so common yet so changing to our experience of life…?

So many alterable chance happenings and so many of what seem to be unalterable precipitants for the future of man act as some sort of universal reagents to the vastness of our experience. Whilst even more so when and if we try to avoid them in the first place.

Little of this magick shines through in any obvious awareness at its moment but its aftertaste lingers and brightens as the finishing vapors of a singular wine leaving its due. Except that is to say, through the discipline of our walking along all of this sometimes incredibly weary path of ours, we will somehow seem to also gain a certain discreet quality to the construct of our own being, that if perseverance serves itself well, lifts us up just a little bit higher than we were but even a short while before.

We all have them. We all experience them. We all ask our own brand of the "why's" to life when we're also knowingly aware that we most likely won't learn a damned thing about most of them immediately.

The old proverb says of the aged soul that "if we could know then, what we know now, we would indeed most likely have lived our lives differently!"

Or would we?

Life isn't served up in reverse order and it never has been. There is no TARDIS or any "Guardian of Forever" for us to worm our way backwards through time so that we might change everything for ourselves!

Life is, because life is, as it is. It's just that simple!

We are born, we learn, we try, and attempt. We challenge, we fail, we try again, and again, and eventually, we somehow achieve and succeed because we just didn't give up on it all!

This is the power of perseverance! It's the reason for the magick of our spirit, and the indomitable strength of our soul!

Bottom line….

Nothing in life ever really comes easily, even those ills we endure.

Nothing is Impossible!

Every morning as the dawn breaks its light and we wake to the greet of the sun, we welcome anew when it shines forth and through, our new day where our Magick gets done!

The same source of power and light living at the center of the sun is that which also shines at the center of our own soul! As the sun provides its incredible life giving creation allowing the renewal of all life and being, so thus are we all capable of such magnificent creation and alteration of our own path of life!

This is why we are so delicately interconnected with the Sun and the moon as with all the stars throughout the heavens!

There IS no separation between us, just bonded intimate interwoven pieces of creation moving and acting unison! This is the true SOURCE of the Magick in all existence!

When you awaken to this, then you come to realize that NOTHING is impossible!

Of Moons and Meanings in All Their Shades!

You'll notice the universe spinning about in certain directions and exerting patterns of force that do indeed have an influence upon people and our world.

You'll feel the energies associated with change casting their eddy's around and against what you have always taken for granted as being usual, ordinary, par-for-the-course for life.

When a full moon rises in the sky, there are effects. When a new moon rises in the sky, there are effects.

When a marked moon rises in the sky and it is interpreted as being one of but a series of signals and indicators in an emerging age in the matters of humankind, the unfortunate case is when few if any allow themselves to pay due attention to their guts, to their intuitions, when so many of their senses are all in concert together about such times.

Then is usually when tides and those forces propelling great change rise and fall leaving only relevance paid long afterwards.

Pay attention to the coming days, they mean something to each of us. For some, great change! For others, great adjustment! For others still,… absolute revelation.

Yes, the sky will darken and the moon will shade its pale, and yes, this will carry meaning. It indicates a doorway that will lead onward as it was always meant to. the thing about doorways however is that while some enter freely and move on through, others choose not to sometimes with a great resistance and an immense amount of struggle.

Pay attention to your intuitions! They will never serve you wrong, no matter who tries to lead you away from them!

Spirits of Protection

Angels pervade the beliefs of the world, from mountains to shores their spirits are heard,
their influence rebounded, their strength has no height, their love is unbound on the wind they take flight.
They greet us every morning and walk in our day, they glee with our fortune, and comfort our dismay.
They gather in with us and our families side too, and guard us each night their devotion so true!
But over all else is their charge and their cast, they'll never give up it's their duty and their last!
So when next you do wonder what power stood your way, what force changed your course, and what influenced your day?
Just try to remember that standing right behind you, are your angels of protection, who are there all right through!

Perceiving Your POWER!

When we tell ourselves that something doesn't exist, what we are really telling ourselves is that we are choosing to not recognize its very existence at all no matter if in fact such a thing is really there or not.

Our senses are an odd little quality to our existence. We see only a minor fraction of the true reality that is all around us. We hear an even smaller fraction of the actual spectrum being projected in the universe. We smell with such variable perception that what one person identifies as a particularly discernable scent, another connects to in an entirely different way of their capacity.

Our soul and its vast perceptive abilities are different however! Oh they are absolutely interconnected and quite intertwined, but they all carry their own diverse characteristics while also integrating themselves into the totality of what we allow ourselves to conclude is our existence.

Our soul is infinite! The reach of its capacity is beyond anything we could even imagine! When we set ourselves to the task of shining its spirit forth from our being, we then begin to get an idea of just what it is we are truly capable of reaching!

You see, when someone tells themselves that they cannot or more precisely that they "will not" see, feel, hear, do, or sense something in their experience of life, what they are actually doing is shutting their senses and their experience down from it. They are choosing to back away from it! Self-creation is shut down in this way. Perceptions of ghosts and spirits are avoided in this way.

Allowing the magick of the spark of creation to emerge along the path of life is altered and dimmed through such a choice. Such a choice is both conscious and non-conscious usually both at the same time in very complex ways. While the etiology of the sources may be complex, the solution however is simple. Just choose to do it and voila', the doorway opens wide!

While we may tell ourselves and others that we want to, or need to "sense", for whatever our reason; we will not sense and perceive and thus to illuminate our ultimate senses until we both consciously and unconsciously unsheathe our spirit and learn to let it move beyond our fears.

Yes, OUR fears!

The fears of feeling what we might actually not want to feel. Those fears of seeing, sensing, and/or perceiving those aspects of existence that once recognized and allowed to "BE" in our reality, then will have to become real to and for us!

Their POWER then manifests into reality!

The trick to all of this is, that once we choose to do this…

SO DO WE manifest our power and our potential into a greater reality!

Have an illuminating passage!

Personal Power is Positively Amazing!!!

It's positively amazing, that most consider themselves so small, so ineffectual, so irrelevant and lacking in their own power, that they really do believe that their own bit of being couldn't be enough to affect incredible alterations onto the fabric of the world!

When if they would just look at history, they would recognize that in the past, all it took was one single soul to set into motion changes and beliefs that served to shift what we now understand as our reality!

Don't think you don't matter!

Purely Magick!

There is Magick born in madness and Magick born from lore, there is Magick lit in gladness and Magick to deplore, there is Magick purely spirit being illuminated from our soul, and that we seek to help us on our path to make us whole.

There is Magick in its season its power forged in spice, and Magick in the undercurrent of all that's good and nice, but the Magick that surpasses all that's spoken of the truth, is that Magick that's bestowed to us, wrought of creation's hoof!

Remembering

Alas my dearest friends, now dims the light of our day and thus enters the strength and the realm we all know as night! As we venture forth and reminisce on the lark of our most recent daily adventures, pray that we will always remember to carry them along with us, for it's largely in the remembering that we draw our conclusions on the beauty of our own being! Venture well through the veil tonight! Love, light, and the brightest of blessings!

Silence…

If you want to know the secret to discovering the Psychic within yourself, then be well advised. That the same place from where we muster every speckle of our Psychic Intuition is also the place from where every bit of Magick that we articulate is formed.

If you think you can handle the revelation of awakening that within yourself; then find it, learn of it, and REMEMBER YOURSELF in absolute SILENCE!

When you awaken this part of yourself you will find that it's in Silence where we find our greatest Power and Strength!

Success Through Self Confidence!

Success is one of those relative concepts that while glaringly objective on the outside, is as much if not so much more subjective in its power and motive on the inside!

Think about it if you will for a moment! If we flaunt ourselves rudely and with as much energy as is possible, no matter how much effort we put forth, in the end what we end up with is a falsehood that shatters to shards!

If however, we dig down deep into our source of doubting and self-recrimination and then decide to cast away any segment of self-damnation that exists, what results is a sudden surge of magnificent emergence in its place! SERIOUSLY!

If you reference any of the literature on the matter of success, one of the things that is common to ALL who drive their way upwards and onwards is that they all do seem to have that common thread of undoubting self-awareness working to their ends!

How do we really infuse such an unfailing sense of self-confidence though? It really is simple! Just take the following three steps!

Every morning before you set off on your way, look yourself in the mirror and in your best and most glowing expression, smile at yourself and then spend a moment thinking: "I AM GOING TO PERSEVERE!"

During the course of your day remember the following!

"I AM GOING TO SMILE and ENGAGE OTHERS COMPLETELY, EVEN IF IT KILLS ME!" – There is nothing more powerful or more convincing to others than a person who is both willing and excited to extend their hand and their strength of spirit on the way toward their goals, especially when they convince others that it is also THEIR common goals as well!

Both throughout your day and at the end of every day close your eyes for a brief moment and recite to yourself that:

"I AM GOING TO BELIEVE IN MYSELF and I AM GOING TO ACHIEVE THIS or (THESE) GOALS NO MATTER WHAT CHALLENGE STANDS IN MY WAY!"

After that, it's all a matter of NOT GIVING UP and making others and creation itself to also have such faith in you!

That's it guys!

Everything after that is a matter of fortifying and continuing your rivers of good ideas, congruent sense of yourself, and remembering the golden rule to successes in this life:

"NEVER, EVER, GIVE UP WHEN YOU KNOW YOU'RE RIGHT!!!"

Now go splash the life fantastic!

Synergy Powering Your Creation

It's a tragic thing the degree to which humankind has dulled their own perspective into the immense gifts that creation has bestowed unto each of us!

The synergy of the soul and spirit, when aligned, has the potential to transmute the power in all that is into all that we are and would be! Just as when one aligns a satellite dish and it receives and projects ALL the signals it is capable of gathering, thus it is with our spirit to our soul receiving and conducting the great energy of creation!

What is That Ultimate Force that IS Creation?
Prayer? Ceremony? Observance?
I know this is a bit long but it is VERY important!
Creation is what resulted from the spark of one ultimate and yet eternal thought! It all began in such a moment. We all, each one of us experience our own lives in a progressive perspective of just such a moment. It's a comprehension of creation parked in a thought yet extended through what emerges in our perspective for what we trust would be, can be, and WILL BE.

Have you ever wondered about all of that talk regarding dimensions, of time, space, of relativity, and just how all of this REALLY works?

Let's suffice it to say then, for the sake of all of this, that everything is right and as all of us have our own way of looking at life, of looking at our world, and as we think about our creation; we all herald our own perspective about our lives. From this, we form what could be, what is yet to be, and what is along our path.

Whether or not you pray to any power other than yourself in all of creation, let's just postulate for a moment that you create nonetheless in just the same way that it would be otherwise. No matter the form of your wishes for yourself and those you care for, life and the path of want-making works just the same no matter how we decide to put it all together for ourselves.

If you tell yourself that there is a God and you believe that your God works in your life, the spirit that formed creation works right along with the force of your soul totally and in an inviolate fashion. If you tell yourself that there is no God, that no power of any such spirit created any and all of this, the ultimate and boundless force that created existence still works right along with the force of your soul, your consciousness if you will just in the same way, in an inviolate fashion.

If you believe yourself to be agnostic, ambivalent, or just not sure, it all works just the same! Creation and all of reality if you will cannot work any other way because if it did, none of this would or could ever be possible because it would have no doubt been eliminated before it could have ever been possible in the first place!

It's part of why there is so much passion and so much energy relating to that substance of thought we call belief! We are you see all aligned in our own way. We all are at least mildly convincing to ourselves as we try to convince others that our way is the best way for ourselves, just as there are others who remain sure that their way of belief is to they, no doubt the best and the "ONLY" way that things are!

Truth be told, and the thing that scares many the most is that ALL ways work just the same, with the same energy, with the same purity, and with the same force of spirit, and that's a cats-tail that few if ever want to grab ahold of where the context of their beliefs are concerned!

Regarding the philosophical side of the power, the spirit, the force, the Magick if you will that created everything and continues to; it remains that humankind has been debating and aligning itself with so many endless forms of thought about its own creation right along with it and this has been changed, adapted, and shifted, and colored in so many tones and tomes so many times that its variations have become almost endless term of abstraction to the very core of our understanding!

In it all, none of it has altered the ability for others to follow their own separate paths, their own ways of belief, their own way of living their lives and experiencing every moment and every emerging experience that they so desire!

It's in the way of creation.

It's written in the very fabric of how and why we are and continue to BE-COME!

Yes, this is also why the substance of creation and its direct advocates like prayer, meditation, ceremony and Magick and so many other forms of petitioning the universe to respond to our desires works the way that it all does!

When we dicker our way down to the bottom line about all of this however, it's ALL a form of:

Thought------------→   directing------------→
Intent.......
And thus Intent------------→ Directing Creation!

When we pray we conduct our spirit with the ultimate spirit that created everything! When those who observe and conduct specific ceremonies, they aren't aligning themselves in supplication or petition to God, the Gods, the universe etc., they are aligning and tuning themselves to a specific cause and effect that simply MUST BE in the manner of creation, no alternative, no pause, no purgatory whatsoever!

When believers in so many various ways of thought all practice and perform their own ceremonies, the grand adjutant cause is again all the same!

The real tickler about all of this is that it's all so simple! It's all so reduced from where it's professed, taught, thought, and imagined to be!

You see, the reality that most of those in any sort of seats of any sort of liturgical or spiritual power don't want you to grasp is that you really don't need a PhD. or a certificate in Theology, the blessings or some bestowal from any other soul in order to bless, invoke, cast protections, to converse with God, the Gods, the Goddess, to ask for help, to beg for change in your life, or however you so identify the Spirit(s).

Every speck of life and each and every instant of your waking and sleeping awareness is an integral part of the entire form of all of the emergence of creation as we can currently perceive it to be for us!

That's the real trick of it all!

The ultimate Magick that IS creation is already written into the very core of the code of creation of our very souls!

And….. it can never, ever, be taken away from any of us! EVER!

Now that's a thought eh?

The Devil Discovered in Deep Rivers!

"Deep rivers run quiet" - Haruki Murakami

You know, I think one of the most difficult positions to embrace on this our dear Mother Earth are those where one must learn and be adept in the art of being a professional moderator, a middle-man, a middle-woman, or "person" if you should so desire.

It's not an easy thing to be good at really! When you come to think about it, its one thing to be standing toward the top of any ladder. It's certainly very difficult to be residing at the bottom of one. Residing in the middle however?

In any group or organizational structure, any family, any gathering mind you taking on the natural task of being well toned and adept at being in the middle of anything is a most difficult place to be.

Not only do you have to be able to field and understand multiple sides of things said, done, and/or expressed and yes, not expressed and theorized about; but you are also asked to be as adept in the practice of communicating and making sound and real so much to so many levels of everyone elses understanding right on and up to the top and all the way down to the bottom and all around.

For that reason alone I've always found myself to be most respectful of that soul and of those souls who are very good at being in the middle, for nobody else really learns and carries such incredible lateral and multi-level talents in such wide fields of their own comprehension!

Yes, it's my utter belief that they should provide Doctoral Degrees for those who are especially good at being in the middle of things, for there are so many others who clearly are not!

In nature we witness everything, yes, "everything" living and existing in some way as a compliment to one another. As things are created, others pass on. As some things are born, others thus die. As some life transitions to its own dawning in one stage of its season, the time eventually comes when it withers and then rests in sleep filled slumber. The ground, leaves, trees, people, and animals are thus! The stars, planets, and the galaxies are just this way!

The energy that makes up the universe, of all things is always active, always alive, always in a state of being! It's quite literally the only thing apart from the complete absence of it that can ever be said to be an infinite constant of its own existence! The rest changes, fluxes, adapts, dawns, and then eventually fades.

We've all frequently heard the phrase "Like a rock", meaning to be sturdy, to be constant, to be enduring. Although as we know, the rock is not always constant, and nor can it be said to be entirely durable. Rocks can melt in extreme high heat, they can be easily broken, they can be degraded and disheveled into a wind-blown dust.

Rocks can also be eroded and washed away by the mere passage of the simple, soft, nature of liquid water over its surface. So is a rock always indeed so durable, so omni-present in our midst? Hardly.

I will say that the sorts of souls who I find myself greatly admiring in this world, are those who appear as being as rocks in their own guise, but who also might be the first to admit that they are anything but as they recognize both their own limitations right along with their abilities. These are usually the same souls who harbor the capacity to integrate the capacities of others in such an understanding way, while also being able to pass these understandings on to others of so many alternating levels and traits.

These are the middle men, the middle women, the adjutants of the excellence of their own omnipresent unanimities.

These are also by the way frequently the very same souls of whom the world has discovered great personal power, of hand, mind, and yes, of Magick of many varied degrees!

These are the souls who frequently express expanded levels of their own consciousness, in their own capacities for comprehension, and in my experience in their own special attuned psychic and mediumship capacities.

These are the souls who usually end up as both being admired as well as vilified. They are the souls who have been historically referred to as being adored and being burned, hung, and yes, crucified for their special traits.

Today, even in our own ascendant way, as we expand our multi-dimensional understandings of ourselves, of our reality, and of our existence, as we both embrace the power of real Magick residing right within our grasp, we also seem to continue to chase away what we see as demons with angels wings from around the corners of every dark tree that we still don't seem to understand.

How easy it is to misjudge the true powers and the very manifest strengths that reside in the currents of those deep rivers within us all.

Some rivers are surely deeper than many others, and as the Magick of existence continues to spark to life and as it begins to encompass all that much more the world used to think of as being so limited, then those rivers will flex their erosive forces with a rapidly accelerating pace upon the world.

Never deny the depths of your own being!

Instead, learn of every level and every cold current that resides within you! For when you do, THEN is when you will begin to command REAL MAGICK IN CREATION!

The Most Powerful Form of Magick!

Would you like to witness the most powerful form of Magick?

It manifests when you center yourself into be-coming ever increasingly empowered, ever more self-aware, endlessly more spirit-aware, and absolutely the most beneficent version of yourself that you can be! Life in this state of LIVING Magick just somehow seems to naturally align with who you are be-coming and who you always were right from the very beginning!

One of the great mysteries in life is that it is a long and winding pathway leading us all to that place where we finally meet our true selves and then to finally shine! This path is as long or as short as you choose and no one route is ever the ONLY WAY!

The Nexus Effect

There is always a path forward. There has always been a path behind. There will always be a way through. There will always be a change to be considered and options that will be overlooked. Very little in life ever stays the same with the one single exception of that spark that resides at the core of us all! Consider it the eternal light of our soul, because that's just what it is!

We are in the presence of an age and a time that has been considered crucial for well over two thousand years of humankind history. Energy does more than indicate, it leads, it influences, it speaks. Spirit does more than preside, it presents and the response indicates the following.

Every now and then there are souls who quite notably influence humankind's way forward. These are people who through their thoughts, actions, and their inactions believe that they are maneuvering the universe to their own ends.

It is however believed that the greater truth is in that as individual paths alter and change, more universal effects come from the compounding of them all leaving individuality as an additive that is as a mere grain on the beach.

What however would be the understanding if we were to understand that when one grain is taken from the beach, everything else is unalterably shifted and can never be returned to its previous state ever again?

Think of this as the effects of one soul upon the entire world!

If one soul were to suddenly shift his or her direction, change his or her mind, to color his or her way suddenly, would this have an effect upon all others and onto the entire world?

Well, there are some souls who by and through their personage for some inexplicable reason just do seem to have such an effect by and for no cause of reason of their own. When such a soul suddenly veers to the right instead of moving to the left, it remains that suddenly others for no logical reasoning has the tendency to also veer off to the right along their way and before you know it, everything has now changed. Why?

This is what's uncommonly and oddly enough referred to in part as "chaos theory" or as I like to call it:

"The Nexus Effect"

Why? Where? How does it work?

Nobody can ever be certain. None that is except to ponder that it does indeed happen.

The deeper and more influential truth is that whether anyone likes it or not; you, I, they, we all, have this effect upon ourselves, on others, on each other, and yes, onto the entire world!

This is why in the grander scheme of things, that individuality does matter!

Singular intent does matter!

How we live and why we choose to be as we are creates the conditions necessary for the magick of creation to work as it always has and as it always will.

Yes, one single soul can change the world! It happens every moment of every day!

If you ever again doubt in the reality of your power to make a difference, and to shift the entire world through your meager footsteps, then remember the power of one single grain of sand to change that beach!

The Power of Undiminished Self Observance

Why is self-observance without judgment considered so high on our collective ladder of awareness? Well, if we as living spirits allow ourselves to rise to the level of being able to look inward deep inside of ourselves as our being resides, without also prejudicing ourselves, we have then removed the filters of segmented understanding, restricted self-viewing, and thus we begin to see just what is there, who we are, what we are, and finally:

ALL THAT WE ARE, period. Truth is that you know what is within you, I know, we all know. We spend a lifetime being taught how to hide away from much of it. Only when we finally remove our tinged capacity for a constant self-diminishment through the constant judgment of all we "think" that we are instead of seeing all that we "truly" are for what it truly is; are we finally released then allow our so-called "intellectual ability" to shift from restricted and on into unlimited!

We learn to love ourselves releasing us. THIS is when we begin to gain a truer perspective about just how much power we hold within ourselves to live, to shine, and to grow into always greater spirits! THIS IS as it was always meant to be for us!

The Quintessence of You!

It's often been said, that the magnificence that we seek is as far as the mind may conceive and as close as the end of our nose. Were it that every soul walking the earth would draw close into themselves and they would awaken to the truth that every bit of a quintessence of what they are, is made up of energy, living energy, all gathered together into a grander expression of being than that of every star in the heavens and every corner in creation! The vastness in all the universe carries nothing when compared to the Magick that is expressed, by all of that, which is expressed in you, right here, right now!

Let us return to a sense of honest social grace between one another that has somehow become forgotten and lost. One that seeks communication and that recognizes a soulful sense of respect. It begins with the parting of your lips, and the tips of your fingers.

The Real Power in Spell-Making!

Edgar Allan Poe said that "words have no power to impress the mind without the exquisite horror of their reality." Perhaps…

To that however I would have to personally add that, "Words contain an infinite and a boundless source of power, both in how they serve to impress the mind, and even more so in how they are capable of adapting and thus, re-creating our reality!"

Spells. How often I've heard this word. How often I've embraced the word! It has the ability to fill some souls with great and biding waves of personal strength and yet, capable of filling others with absolute feelings of dread. The tides of its inferences have in the distant past sent poor souls to the stake and the pyre, and even today, parts of the world still harbor archaic prejudices with that of the power of the spell.

When I'm asked about spell-making and regarding my own personal Magickal practices I usually keep any revelations relating to the labors of my own artwork to a bare minimum if at all. I do reveal that I follow ancient paths and practices as well as invoking a sense of common day and age sense of spirit!

I walk in the footsteps of the ancients, those of my ancestors, of the Viking fires and the ceremonial circles of the Britain's. I walk the path of the Hermetic, I study the science of nature, walk with the ancient spirits of the Greeks and the Egyptians, and I walk in the paths of the Celtic Gods and Goddesses. Yes, it's all described in a rather broad brushstroke, but the truth is after all usually an infinite quality of expression.

Spell-making is a thing that I rarely discuss openly due to the impact of my beliefs and how I see them being reviewed in open terms by others. The wider truth as I see it and as some who have come before me is that everyone in their own way practice the art of some form of "spell-making".

This no doubt would be viewed as divisive by some and even more so offensive by others. I beg a bit of abstract thought however if you will. For in the minds of many a practitioner, the cold and hard fact is that any time someone utters a plea to the vestiges of creation, to their understanding of God, to the Gods, the Goddesses, they are in some way invoking the spark of the powers of a spell!

In recent day's popular wordplay has been made in that "the forming of words is in its own way a form of spell making, which is why it's called spelling!"

This may just be truer than many might like to believe! The same manner of altering the vexing nature of it is increasingly witnessed as it's being more popularly now referred to as invoking "The Law of Attraction." Same coat. Different colors and styles. More controversially, in terms more common, the very nature of prayer is in itself a form of spell making. It's an invoking of the ultimate spirits in the soul of creation to make true people's wants and needs, and to plead with the powers of creation for better lives and for a better world. Although there are plenty of figures who would themselves consider such views heretical and placed in even worse terms, the bare truth remains.

None of this is intended to threaten any one or more ways of belief. In fact, if anything, these words are intended to further broaden the brush-stroke of a common understanding that might emerge between so many of various ways of belief, though even I admit, such avenues are no doubt wishing for miracles.

Remain it for me to say that as I see it, the true power that's contained in and throughout ALL of spell-making, no matter what the system or the manner of belief, no matter what shade of light or of darkness, or what color of the mind is that this power, the power that adapts, shifts, that recreates the nature of being, always begins with the realm of the Gods and ends with the spark of our own thoughts and how we channel these to the nature of that realm we call our sense of being.

Let's not forget that it was Nicola Tesla who said he was absolutely certain that there was an ultimate intelligence at the very center of the universe, and while he had yet to reach it, he was always certain that it was there and that it touched us!

In layman's terms, what he was referring to in my view was that the same source and spark of the ultimate river of knowledge that continues to unfold from the nature of creation, is itself always right at our feet and tapping at the edges of our minds! Every one of us, one-by-one, drawing in its power, invoking of its character, and adapting and re-creating the nature of our existence one little bit at a time!

THIS is the nature of ALL Spell-Making!

We all invoke our vision, our understanding, and our shifts in our nature of reality! We all in some way reach out and touch of God, the Gods, the Goddess(es), at every bend and corner that is the ultimate expression of the ultimate spirit that is creation! We study the science of nature, and of every aspect of its spice and leaf, of every article of its light, in it's shades of greys, in its colors, and of its darkness. It is all a voice of creation we all both listened to and what we respond to.

In this way, perhaps if you are one who tends to cast aspersions against those who seem to reside on what you see as the extreme fringes of belief, those of "Pagan Worship", the Witches and the Warlocks, those who seek and practice the art of spell-making in their own manners of belief; perhaps you just might take a moment to also remember, that even in your own way, you are also affecting your own understanding of your sense of creation with the yearnings you put out there in front of you in your own way!

It ALL is a part of the power of what you see as God, that which created all of what is!

It ALL is a form of Spell-Making!

Yes, I recognize that the last line is the one that many won't claim kin to!

The Safer Path Will Usually Get Your No-Where!

What if you had the opportunity to take a turn in life that might forever ruin any sense of a professional career but could also serve to illuminate your sense of self?

What if you faced a point in your life when you could choose to stand alone against all odds facing a storm, risking the loss of friends, family, and any conventional sense of professional respect, if it would also ensure that the remainder of your life would also be spent in a true path of service to humanity?

What if you were given the choice to decide to withdraw into a wilderness for a protracted time, if it would also help you to unfold the mysteries of the spirit?

We all arrive at some opportunity in our life where we might break the bonds of conventionalism and lift the curtain on some grander way of being! The question is: would you seek out such revelation, or choose the safer more acceptable path in your life? Our own particular steps to heaven and hell.

One of those quintessential visions we have all adopted regarding the great beyond is that of the rising stairway leading us up to the realm of heaven!

There are reasons that this has been throughout our span of being. One is the extension of our spirit to that realm beyond the veil that we have all felt and experienced throughout our existence. Another is our integral understanding of the ascendance of our soul after our physical death. Yet another is the ascent of our conscious awareness to that state of being that disbands many if pray, "all", the old shackles and constraints that we've felt bound by throughout our lives.

There are many reasons that people hold onto this iconic form as their most common conception about the ascendance to that ultimate realm of the spirit after our death. Above all else however is this…

Perhaps, just perhaps, aside from all of the givens, the presumptions, the lectures and liturgical sermons that we have endured, and so many more that led us to where we are right now in our lives, it might just be that it's because we also associate this vision with our rising and re-joining with all of that of ourselves that we have always known exists. Could it be that we in some way have always felt that we somehow left some part of ourselves behind?

When we allow ourselves to ascend these steps and to move onward onto the level of that existence where we feel we truly belong, we are doing more than reacquainting ourselves with ourselves. We are realigning and completing our own inner vision of some parts of ourselves that we have up until now in this life denied of ourselves!

In essence, we "BE-come" again and the results of this are the absolute MAGICK of the spirit!

In our world today it's easy to begin to feel like we're getting lost in all of the chaos, the difficulty, and into all of the personality antics that are hallmarking our age.

Proponents of many ways of belief are all signaling that we are in an age of ultimate challenge, of trial, which at least on the surface seems to be a fair assessment.

Underneath all of the chaos, the dark tides, and the social meandering that is spanning the globe there is a light that is lit for each of us. Some of these lights reside across fields of intense experience. Some of these lights sit mounted upon carriages that are moving along with us traveling those many pathways we navigate. Some of them are peeking over the edge of tomorrow, as a sail mast making its way toward us over the farthest edge of what seems to be an endless sea upon the earth, and others still, reside right in front of us leading our way to a stairway that for its own reason is always poised to lead us onward and upward no matter what or how we try to avoid its meaning for us.

Every path, every way of life, all of the experiences we include into our storehouse of footsteps are all islands that we form for ourselves. They are islands that we choose to continually visit, and they are lands that once we've had enough, we eventually depart heading for other lands along our way.

Yes, we make mistakes. We make plenty of them! None of us are perfect in this by any means although we personify the perfection of the spirit and of the soul at our core that is who and what we truly are.

We walk, we live, we reach and we yearn to constantly ascend that stairway that is always leading us upward, ever higher, with each experience, with each success, with each achievement, and with each failure. It is a pathway of true revelation!

Each time we stumble and fall and then rise again, we reach up even higher! Each time we try, sometimes we succeed, and then more frequently we fail again and again, in some other way we are reminded that we are fallible and while we eventually are humbled by our failures, we never stop striving to rise up from the ashes of our failures and to fly with eagles above the clouds!

This is what is meant by seeking the Magic in your quest for life! Because we are all on some form of a "vision quest" as many of the ancients and as the Native Americans describe of it.

Howsoever you choose to set your feet upon the pathway of your life, whether it be along a brightly lit venue or that of twilights keep. Be your path wading through the darkness of our age or if you set your steps onto a solitary journey of wonder and illumination, we are all in our own way, eventually, heading ourselves to rejoining with that part and those parts of ourselves that we set out from in order to come here and to try, to do, and to be everything and everyone we have chosen to!

Difficult it is to grasp for some that no matter what you do, who you are, what you experience, and what you achieve and what you fail at, that we are all headed back to that same set of steps on the stairway to our own ultimate existence.

Work the Magic of your spirit, of your soul in your own way and embrace it for all you are!

Don't deceive yourself however…

Eventually, sometime, somewhere, somehow, we will ALL stand before some form of that same stairway, and in the end moments of all of this, of our own days here, we will all return to that dawning from whence we did set out from in the first place…

The Understandings of the Ancients

I was recently struck by a series of statements I heard by a Dr. Juliette Wood of Cardiff University England as she spoke relating to the mythological and the historical impact that the figure known as Merlin has had upon history and cultures worldwide.

One of the factors that immediately occurred to me in her oration was that it was in her view and thinking, that Dr. Wood almost ideally related her statements of Merlin and what was then understood as Magick to the very core of the fabric of modern Magick and its interwoven connectedness to modern spiritual belief. To this she said and I quote:

"To the age of Merlin, ritual Magick was accessing something beyond human where now in the 21st century we are all in a period where we feel disconnected and we are seeking…" Referring to the Magick of the age of Merlin as we all romantically tend to relate to it now in both a metaphysical sense and in a very spiritual sense, she said that:

"It isn't just the wisdom of science, it's the wisdom of science and more…"

"It isn't just the wisdom of Paganism, it's the wisdom of Paganism, and more…"

"It isn't just the wisdom of Christianity, it is much more!"

I often find myself coursing about my own studies and my own revelations on the philosophy of modern life and of Magick and remembering how many times I've heard it expressed, very passionately mind you, that in our world today, we seem to have forgotten so much more than we could ever possibly recall.

I ponder on the wealth of knowledge and the understandings that must have indeed been grasped by the ancients in so many deeper and more intimate ways than most of we in our own age would even allow of ourselves?

Those of us who strive to walk the path of the spiritual and of Magick do indeed seek to strive to grasp that fabric that is the interconnectedness that exists between what we now comprehend as the wisdom of science and so much more that surely exists beyond our current capacity to understand!

How much is it even considered of that wisdom that the ancients grasped and celebrated in what we today refer to as modern Paganism; and how would we embrace our own personal path should we unfold those understandings in the intimate ways as the ancients once did?

How many times has it been said that virtually every modern expression of faith and belief owes its roots in, to, and is directly affected by the influences of all that we today call the age and the beliefs of the ancients?

I find myself almost celebrating the words of Dr. Wood and I think one addition to my personal "wall of phrases fame" will now certainly include these words:

"To the age of Merlin, Magick was accessing something beyond human where now in the 21st century we are all in a period where we feel disconnected…"

We more than ever in recent times are beginning to accept that where Magick is concerned:

"It isn't just the wisdom if science, it's the wisdom of science and more…"

"It isn't just the wisdom of Paganism, it's the wisdom of Paganism, and more…"

"It isn't just the wisdom of Christianity (and of so many other ways of thought), it is so much more!"

Good words…

Through the Gateway

There are some days and some moments in creation that are more charged, more conducive to change and alteration, just different! These as Thomas Paine said so poetically "are the times that try men's souls..."

Not because of conflict or of struggle, but because they allow us to propel ourselves beyond the boundaries of our own imagination! Every so often we are given a doorway, a gateway, a nexus over which we might transcend our own doubts and move into another state of absolute brilliance!

What keeps some from moving over that nexus? Their own self-doubts and inability to open up their minds to their own possibilities in existence!

The rest however WILL choose to move on despite the others. It is these souls who will craft the future! Choose to "BE" one of them!

Touching the Face of Eternity

There will come that time one day when as you close your eyes and delve within, suddenly awareness shines as never before. You find yourself standing transfixed before eternity itself!

No longer in awe or mystique, but merely gazing over what is and always has been leading up to the edge of your path. Here in the rubric of your destiny you no longer mourn or yearn, you no longer have others along with you, but instead, you hear and witness the presence of eternity tenderly touching your cheek and your soul and you learn that you were always intended to reach this point along your way!

Don't mourn the passage of friends as they seek their own path now. Don't grieve over things that no longer serve any purpose to you or your path. Instead, touch the face of eternity in return and allow yourself to finally recognize that it is and always was within you all along right from the very beginning!

Have a beautiful night everyone!

Trusting in Yourself is a Source of Incredible POWER!

It's one of those qualities that we all deeply desire and spend more time trying to fulfill, almost more than any other in life.

Trust.

The mere mention of the word can sound like an abstract utopian vision sketched in our idea of the passage of our lives while also endearing visions of the waves of so many stormy seas.

While we could easily draw up a Blog post as long as our arm on trust, that isn't the purpose of my bringing it up here, in this humble space.

The sort of trust that I'm referring to right now is the brand that affects us in such an elementary way! Because whether any of us want to admit it or not, how much we choose to trust ourselves, in our momentary thoughts, in our feelings, in our plans, our dreams, in those gut intuitive stretches of our imagination that have a very real and a direct bearing upon our morning, our day, our week, and yes, a direct bearing upon our lives, this trait is more creative of us all than we would ever want to think!

I remember reading a passage about George Washington and his own dilemma on one cold winter night. It was on the west banks of the Schuylkill River at Valley Forge and just twenty-two miles from British held Philadelphia in the bitter winter of 1777-1778.

General Washington was dug in staying with his forces trying to set about to the task of winning a struggle that would either serve to craft a nation or reduce all hopes of freedom into a defeat without measure. It hadn't been going well for them all with a long string of defeats.

I recall reading that one evening General Washington sat quietly at his desk in front of a modest fire and in his deep thought, he found himself struggling to believe in what he knew he had to do in order to move things forward for his men and for the war again.

General Washington was having a moment of despair in any sort of faith in himself and of his abilities. He had to face facts. Many of his men were sick, some lay dying, and some even more at the point of starvation for the lacking of supplies and he needed to do something drastic about it.

The General knew that what he needed was a miracle of faith in his own sense of vision and planning that would move things forward again and he didn't have much time in order to do it.

Washington was in a momentary state of great lacking in trust in himself.

What finally dawned upon Washington in that moment was that what was needed was to muster himself and then to inject a rising hopeful spirit into his men! The soldiers who remained with him were there and stayed there because they were all Patriots who truly believed in their cause and Washington was under no fool impression.

He knew very well that he was blessed to have such a group of men who somehow retained faith in him! It was therefore his duty to meet to their vision and to rise the challenge. He prayed, long and dutifully, he prayed for strength, for vision, and for a sense of spiritual fortitude!

As History would report it, along with the help of his Prussian military adviser Frederick von Steuben, Washington then kept his men busy, he activated their minds with drills and the strategies of modern military engagement techniques, and drove them onward in hope and self-trust in their cause. It was a practice in creative vision that in the end, served both he and his men well!

Washington helped his men to believe that they would indeed persevere! In the end it served to convince himself as well and it gave him great strength! By continually convincing both they and he of their capabilities, they all found their way to an unswerving path of trust! The brand that was required to craft a spirit of unassailable hope! The type that creates miracles!

It worked and it worked well!

After their departure from Valley Forge, things began to change in the Continentals favor.

The energy of their self-will and their self-determination was unleashed and allowed to create the paths and the venues that were necessary to achieve what they had set out to do!

Against all of the odds and to the absolute dismay of British General Lord Cornwallis, who had little to no respect for what he referred to as "mere farmers with their pitchforks"; Washington and the American Army beat their way to their cause.

Trust won out!

This is the sort of trust that I refer to today. Trust in yourself. Trust in your feelings. Trust in your dreams. Trust that somewhere, somehow, someplace, deep within you, all that you know you are and all that you are capable of is more than just a fleeting vision of hope or despair!

Trust in yourself and who you know yourself to be, releasing and setting ablaze to the whims and the detriments of all others who would try to tell you otherwise!

Sometimes one of the hardest of things that any of us can do is to look ourselves in a mirror and to tell the soul looking back to really and truly trust!

Because when you can unlock that power and the Magick contained in really and truly trusting that potential that is within you, NOTHING AND NO ONE can ever stop you!
As Washington discovered.

Tuning the Spirit in Stradivari Fashion

It's a difficult affair to try and tune a Stradivarius violin amidst a cacophony of other instruments all making their own bits of incredible noise. The way to tune any such instrument is in a place of silence. The tune and tone of your spirit is absolutely no different! Thus will we fully appreciate the magnificence of its beauty!

Unstoppable Power!

It's always been a rather amazing thing you know! As beings we've always retained the ability to reach into eternity and to ponder all that we understand as reality, and yet, we continue to stubbornly abstain any dimensional understanding about the almost infinite capacity for power, strength, and creation that we all harbor within ourselves! All that is until somehow we finally learn it for ourselves!

Then we suddenly become an unstoppable force to the amazement, the wonder, and the frequent fears of many others!

Walking Each Other Home!

We live our days all paths we take some rise then others fall, from young to old, from meek to bold, embracing of them all! Hard working strain and play in vain all moving onward do, but in our vast and spanning ways we're different right straight through. Though with all this and surely more there's one great common tome, it's through our days in separate ways we're walking each other home!

A Spark of Mother's Magick!

Greetings good souls and dearest friends on this fine day!
A special bit of Magick will be spoken this day, to bring sparks of wonder and much love your way! Your devotion has been legend, your selfless care of us so true, we would hardly be the same, without your love to see us through!

Today we call upon Lord Father God and the Mother Goddess to bestow blessings of peace, health, happiness and goodwill to all of the Mothers in the world who have made a difference in all of our lives!

At Parnassus!

Alas dearest ones, as the day winds down and the eve takes its time, the things yet to do in life begin to truly rhyme. Itineraries grow and their implementations loft, the flighty often grab and the easy casually soft.

But as the night comes on and as we ponder on our paths, we madly seek our meaning as we rather make our math. Then oddly as we nestle in our nightly settled beds, and we softly sink on down into very comfy wrapping sheds, we loosen our bodily gates and then float off into the sails, as we cross our ways beyond this world and on through parted veils.

Its there we meet with spirits and we face Parnassus themes, we give our life true meaning and we set our paths on dreams. We choose our way on forward from enlightened brimming thoughts, and then come back down to earth where then we make our patterns wrought.

From there the setting made to do is up to us in might, and we then set our steps on forward seeing that it turns out right! The thing that we must see to so that all our lives will be, is to keep our gazing attitudes as fluid as the sea! For then the magick will emerge and manifest at large, and we'll live the lives we beckon for and do it at a charge!

Alas Awareness Brings Power as Life!

Alas dearest souls the time has come to settle the day's events, as twilight brings anticipated things, that fill our hearts all spent. As all we yearn in what we've learned of world and fabric and life, will all be stored in box and board while spirit seeks enchanted things rife.

The quality of the veil above that seeks our presence and strength, sublime fulfills our deepest thrills of being, existence, and length! The proof you seek contained in reach beyond all proper or vain, resides in one, the mere undone, for nothing you've gained is plain.

The more you seek the wider you peak and suddenly the whole world's changed, those around you know by how you glow that something within you has ranged.

But you are sure by all that's pure of all

your senses enhanced, your reception aglow, your spirit does flow, your insight intuition not chance.

The greatest of things that time will bring into your steps and stride, twill awareness bring light, beyond your night, magickal wonder becomes your ride!

The thing about opening wide the doorway of your own awareness is that once it's opened, what follows, is enlightenment and enchantment beyond compare!

Then my dearest ones, everything changes!

All Fog Banks Pass!

Occasionally the fog sets in somewhere along the path of life! When we find ourselves set into an imposing bank of fog, the first thing that most common sense thinkers do is to slow themselves down and begin to gauge their passage along their way the best that they can because no longer can they see where their going. Fear not however!

Where the matters of your soul and spirit are concerned, there is always a beacon of light shining itself through the thick mist always there to lead you to clearer waters and safer paths!

If however you close your spirit off to this eternally lit lighthouse for your soul, eventually it will find a way to break through to you anyway.

You will however save yourself much trial along your way if you would only just keep your senses open and allow yourself the passage that leads out of the fog! All fog banks pass and once again we all will find ourselves in clear skies again!

An "Island" You're Not!

Empathy as defined is a character trait that alludes to the vicarious experiencing of the thoughts, feelings, and/or attitudes of another person.

If we all were to approach each of our days living our lives and going about our respective tasks while also keeping a small yet pronounced section of our conscious awareness to the experience of others who are around us, we might benefit an abundance of insight into the reality that others who we encounter also have their own goals, their own dreams, their own struggles, their own happiness, and fears, and trepidations, and challenges through every one of their days as we do ourselves.

It's all too easy to just pass off the experience of others as being irrelevant to what we are currently going through, but the truth is that when we remain attuned and sensitive to the experience of others while attending to our own, it makes us much more insightful, much more intuitive, more sensitive, it makes us better team players, more qualified leaders, better coworkers, and a hell of a lot more sensitive and caring as a member of our own family!

This not to say we should try to be perfect at anything, but, a bit more attendance to these qualities will make us more congruent of ourselves and our own experience if we don't' dispel of the experience of others moving in our sphere in our lives!

Are You a Teacher of Your Own Soul?

All too often we tend to focus our collective energies on the fabric of the altered ills that we imagine can unfold in our lives, instead of focusing our creative energies upon all that can unfold along those brighter and more magnificent paths awaiting us!

When you choose the path of focusing your thoughts upon disorder, chaos, and those darker tidings you are taught to accept as the "real world", of course you will eventually find some devil residing behind every tree and doorway you cross.

If however you pull back the veil away from the light that resides within you, its potential and magnificence are so great that it has the capacity to turn you away from this bad creative habit and to manifest incredible results in your life!

Once you choose such a way, suddenly there will be those who will raise their eyes and notice and then they will want the same for themselves! This is the reason so many teachers are currently needed, and yes, if you are reading this and if you find that it tweaks something veiled inside of your soul, then you are one of them!

CAST THE PAST INTO THE WINDS OF OBLIVION!

One of the most intrinsic of global experiences that we all face along our living path is that we will all feel beset with challenges that we wonder if we'll ever make it through and prevail. The past tends to seem as a chain around our necks affecting the clarity of our present and thus we become convinced that it is always diminishing our ability to clear the mist from a future we would otherwise create!

The truth is that, as you have all read time and again, the past is gone, done, finite' and now, in this moment, is all of the Magick of existence we all require to CAST THE PAST INTO THE WINDS OF OBLIVION!

Our future is always an infinite state of magnificent wonder yet to emerge, and how it unfolds precisely is a matter of the choices and the decisions we make and what we all do right here and now!

Don't let the past determine your present choices and actions!

You are no longer the soul you were yesterday!

You are the soul you are today and the future IS "always in motion" and has yet to be cast and manifested into the here and now!

Believe it!

Dealing with Judgments!

There was a wise soul who once said that "If one responds to a publicly demonstrated lackluster judgment by another, then power is given to they and to it." If you know that such freestyle opinion-flinging has no basis in reality relating to you, then the wisest thing to do is to let it fall to its own eventual demise."

I agree intimately with what Sir Anthony Hopkins has to say on the opinions of others. He stated that:

"My philosophy is, it's none of my business what people say of me and think of me. I am what I am and I do what I do." This is the philosophy of the Church of the Devil.

Further I would personally add to Mr. Hopkins feelings on this matter by stating that:

"If what I do serves the better good of others in the world, then so be it.

If however what I do does not serve others, in one way or another, then I would probably never hear their opinions in the first place. In either eventuality, walking on eggshells along my path waiting for the judgments of others is not a very sound or a very productive way to live ones life.

Not to mention the degree of attention it takes away from living up to being the best and the fullest that I can be!"

To be.

At our greatest unrestrained.

Destiny

Destiny is a funny olde thing! The more that people chase it injecting their own sense of greed, want, and abusive manipulations, the more that they will encounter continuing difficulties of all sorts that end up more like blockades than adjustments along the way.

I've always marveled at those souls who spend their time chasing some quality of life that their own mind they conceive as "greatness" when in the end, they are simply never happy with what they gain through their machinations!

When however we travel down our path seeking to better our lives, seeking to better the lives of others, and to make better all that we encounter, oddly enough destiny ends up falling right into our laps and for all of the struggle and manipulations we might have exerted to get there, we end up being better people for the final effects!

Try thinking a little bit about your path today and if and why have you been struggling for each step you take versus having instead been trusting of yourself to be the best that you can be and if you have been encouraging this in all others you encounter? I think you'll find that it does make a difference!

Then tonight as you set your head down on your bed and ready yourself for bliss, allow your means, their skylight beams, and part the veil with this!

Remember, you can't raise yourself up by assassinating the characters of those you hold resentments against! You can't achieve true success by veiling the accomplishments of others.

You can't help yourself to feel more at peace with yourself by making yourself so busy you won't have the time to attend to what's really going in inside of you, and, you won't discover your true path in life by always following in the footsteps of others as they move along their own.

Be a rebel!

Walk down a path nobody has traveled before and find yourself there!

This is the Devil's Path. The path of ultimate illumination!

Discover the Path to Your Destiny!

To look into your future, try to leave the past behind, if your pondering the present try no retrospect to find, if your seeking bright enlightenment try opening the gate, and if swinging wide awareness, look within for no escape. If your focusing on spirits, try to calm your skin unfurled, for to seek of them is one thing but inclusion is the word.

To ask for illumination and awareness is as natural as ice, but when we'll all usually find them is when taking their advice. There's nothing left in hatred that can ever help your toil, and there's nothing good in bitterness to weed your garden soil. But when seeking of that Magick that will make your path emerge, seek that voice of bright enchantment that sparks your spirits surge!

Then when daily you awaken try to focus on your spice, and when readying all your bedtime, lay your head down peacefully nice! Because in all your goals and all your dreams and all your hopes so true, alas the source of manifesting Magick comes all right inside of you!

May you pass through to illumination tonight and chart the path to your destiny!

Do You Believe in the Magick Manifested by your Soul?

Somewhere along the road of our lives we all reach a point when we realize that something has been guiding our footsteps and shielding us along our way.

The sense is unmistakable!

It's a perception of an energy, a spirited presence that should we simply lower our walls and pay attention to what we know to be true instead of that we're all told is true, then our own soul would permeate the perception that we are indeed a part of a grand collection of a great, of an ultimate consciousness that allows for us to live, to create, and to experience!
We live and build our experiences along our path through the Magick that is manifesting our reality! Individually we make strong Magick whether we believe it or not. When we believe it, and accept it, and then focus our spirits upon all of those resources that we've been given, of nature, of the universe, of the Gods, then NOTHING is beyond our capacities! The key is contained in one thing and one thing alone! BELIEF!

Belief is our lighthouse keeper that always has a guiding light shining for us in all storms, in all weather, in fog and in rain, in dead of night and in the sun and clear blue sky of the day!

Do you believe in the Magick manifested by your soul? If not don't feel all so bad. You're not alone. Most don't either.

Be different. Be powerful.

Choose to be and then see.

In for a Penny, In for a Devil's Pound?

Well my dearest ones, as we all resurrect our adoration for the presence of the sun, the moon, of light and the gates of darkness, we must also nary forget to embrace the strength of the moon and the universe that guides our spirits in the night!

"In for a penny in for a pound", exerted efforts to bring us round is what was said to pacify our move, when few withstood the make of wood for altered byway bakes that settled most motions though could lose. There's little in the way of a chance and taken stay for the resigned standing back beyond the wire, for the only real set way to get into all the flay is to point your nose and kick up toward the fire!

To grow in the face of power and then spark that eternal dove it means being daring and to also choose, for if you sit back fine on your laurels knitted thine, then for sure you will only find your groove.

So tonight as lay you do on your pillow ruffled through and you ponder on the meaning of your path, just close fine of your eyes and then do dare to think of nine, and then fear not of the veil or through for you!

The problem with always thinking of casting your spell meant to open wide your path, is that for it to become an effective mover in your life you must be willing to also cast action through your spirit in the direction of your path for it to mean anything!
The path must be moved upon, not only cast!
In for a Devil's pound!
Nothing less!

Journey to Your Undiscovered Devilish Realm!

There are places in our midst, of which, none other paint a picture as calm and exciting nor as arduous and as peaceful as the dark and light in our soul. Think of the places you have frequented in your life that served to somehow set you apart from all others. Those places that have cast their mark, set a brand onto your spirit that for their color and the threads of their character changed your forever.

I've always thought of places like Transylvania, Chicago, or New Orleans, of Hollywood, or of Salem Massachusetts as among the few of those places I have frequented that made them in part between the gathering of that "the undiscovered country, from whose bourn no traveler returns…".

Our lives tend to be a journey of constant discovery, up until that moment when we all will embark upon that ship that carries us onward yet still to an even greater journey. The voyage never ends! Thus our enthusiasm for the passion of life never ends either!

No matter what has unfolded in your past or is unfolding right now! Be it pleasure or pain, passion or perseverance, every moment and every place, every person and every situation has an effect upon us. But when we meet with that shaded and cloaked figure of destiny at the crossroads of that one place, that one "Undiscovered Country" where we become changed forever, this is when we become indoctrinated among the Illuminati, the enlightened, the aware, and this is when our lives will never, ever, be the same ever again!

Knowledge and Wisdom!

Alas my dearest ones, along the trek of everyday life we live and meek in oration, though settled we do when our daytime is through endeared we are of oblation.

No matter how far we've sought of the par between that we know and we would, it resides in the mind of the soul who in-kind knows that knowledge and wisdom if could.

For the way through the veil send us far from our hail of grapeshot that the world sends somehow, even if knowing learns from living worldly of some, through the veil is the wisdom en mews.

So when next you do plea for some way do to see of the trueness and meaning of wise, do remember that you see yonder veil land we'll be, of that wisdom we gain every night!

The Devil's Might is the Light-Bringers RIGHT!

Lately I've been reminded of the importance of being aware of our own global perspective and that how we think we are interpreting people, situations, and our world can and does draw us into reconcilable misunderstandings with ourselves once we open ourselves up to the possibility that we might not be seeing things for what they truly are or how we would instead have them be!

It's important to remember to stop ourselves occasionally, and to close our eyes, and then to breathe calmly before reasserting our senses to all of the people, the places, and the things we have surrounding us. Remember!

We can be both our own greatest resource and sometimes our own worst enemies when it comes to our perspectives! See things both for what they are and for how you would rather they "BE" in your life!

If you want upset and ill in your world, that's easy! If you want revelation, brilliance and absolute MAGICK to emerge, well, that's just as easy too!

JUST BELIEVE IT and then MAKE IT BE in your perspective!!!

Manifesting AWESOME!

Fridays are usually a day that everyone looks forward to! A day to wear loose fit dress down clothes at work. Perhaps it's a good time to enjoy a fun lunch or a trip out after work with coworkers?

You have a whole weekend to look forward to! In and amidst all of everything that is happening in your life, and in anticipation of all you have to look forward to, don't ever forget that one personal vision that charges up the energy of your spirit and that releases your ultimate potential! It's wrapped up in truly believing this connected phrase!

"I AM AWESOME!"

Believe it! Live it! Manifest it!

Let it BE and let your spirit fly free!

Then run with it every moment of every one of your days and watch what happens!

Meet Your Truth in the Darkness with the Devil's Shadow!

Alas my dearest ones, as the cask of night lowers onto our eyes and the midnight moon paints its shade blue, the ridge of the path that we all have ahead gets a rest from our thought-making new.

Whether made up of hollow in the dead of the night or we find ourselves walking alone, down an odd natured way set in a frightening way, all the more will we ponder our tome. For the truth that resides deep where all mostly hide is that insight meets truth in the dark, there where hidden things rise and then odd spirits fly to the freedom they all find in this lark.

So when next you allay all your days tiring play and your seeking some solace through truth, just remember its there in the nighttime so fair and the veil that invites us in sooth!

Meeting the Power of Creation!

The source of your spirit is the power of the world expressed in its grandest possible surplus, though minor is our cue showing us the whole way through, it resides in our soul marking our purchase. When the time is in line and all ready at the start you will know of your true and honored path, it's the power of the soul formed in spirit shown in whole, and just then all is when you'll gain your purpose!

Deep down within each of us is a key to a doorway releasing our true potential!
This is the very thing that most establishments of common religion would like us to deny.
Thankfully, not that of the Church of the Devil.
Once turned and opened, it is a passage that will never be closed again for it feeds us the charged frequencies that create the universal power of ultimate creation and the adaptation of all of creation in our midst!

Of Legends and Legacy!

Perhaps as the eastern traditions have taught, the most important of things we could ever expect to carve of ourselves into the imprint of the history of the world is to add the best and the most

Legacy! We all in our own way, do hope and pray, that along someday, we would all leave behind us in the living wake of our lives some form of a legacy of ourselves, an imprint of our moment here, some meaning that was carved by us throughout our existence while we were here.

It's not a new theme of life you know. As far back as humankind goes, at least in some meaningfully romantic and esoteric sense, humankind has always sought to leave something of ourselves behind after we depart for lands beyond the sea of life.

Perhaps "what" we leave behind us in our path isn't really as important as the "qualities of being" that we have painted while being here?

As we live many of us get all caught up into getting, gaining, acquiring, possessing, controlling, commanding, and manipulating all of what we can in order to create things as 'WE" wish them to be.

Perhaps as the eastern traditions have taught, the most important of things we could ever expect to carve of ourselves into the imprint of the history of the world is to add the best and the most magnificent of ourselves to the beauty, to the natural flow, to the Feng-Shui of the universe as a result of our individual presence?

We all have affected the lives of someone in our days, of others, we all have changed the world just a bit due to our being here if even in the slightest of ways. If we move a pebble on a beach as we walk along its calm and serene setting, does this mean that we have changed it unalterably and left something of ourselves that will live on through the ages in our absence?

If each of us chose to move a pebble, or a bit of sand on this same beach through our days however through the path of our collective lifetimes, what then would the presence of this beach portray to the universe?

Yes, we all have a lasting effect upon the world, and upon the lives of others no matter how much or how little we think we have done along our way!

Perhaps if we all seek to merely shine at our most brilliant as we live our lives, doing what we can at our best for ourselves and others, and through this trusting that what we leave due to this living effort, we will leave a bit of the best of ourselves?

Today, as you move about, as you view the old buildings and the new, as you think on the lives that were lived, the sacrifices, the losses, the trials and the triumphs that were made by those who built, those who created, those who nurtured and those who moved on, remember that you too are right now leaving your imprint upon this place where legends were born!

This is worth continuing a smile today yes?

One Timeless Rule!

There is one cardinal and timeless rule that has always existed in the universe. It is a primal condition that was in place when the thought that brought about the formation of the fabric in all of what is first came to be.

It is the principle basis that first allowed the stars to form, the planets to take shape, and allowed the reaction of the very first organism of our world to spring to life eventually becoming all of that which you see right here and right now!

It is the causal link that formed and allowed the chain reaction that brought about creation! This dynamic allows the strings of creation to vibrate at and to an infinite range of interactive frequencies that form what we call the adaptive fabric of reality.

Its dynamics allow us to shift and change it. It allows that which some call Magick to take place! It is the same basis for what some affectionately refer to as "The Law of Attraction!" It is the spirited dynamic that allows every electrochemical and neural reaction to form and happen and that allows the physicality of bodily essence, presence, motion, our integrated physical response, and the adaptive changing of the basis of all life!

This cardinal rule is most easily understood by absorbing and interpreting the following! When you do understand it, intimately, then you will understand why all things are as they are, up to and including our passage through and beyond the veil of this life!

"Through teaching others we learn best of that which we teach. Through service to others we gain the quality of that which we give. Through magnanimity to others who wrong us, we gain the forgiveness we have sought most importantly from ourselves for so long. Through helping others to heal, we are ourselves healed. Through giving we also gain! Through the formation of a thought is the essence of the presence of another thought that causes yet another. When a thought is formed, it causes creation to adapt, and that's simply the elementary truth to the dynamics of our existence!"

Our Emerging Self Destruction!

"Just as a snake sheds its own skin, we must shed our past over and over again." - Buddha

This process need not be one motivated of a darker spiritual despair, though in many cases this is the proponent that causes it to come about. It need not be the result of outside influences forcing us onto certain avenues of action, though in many cases this is a proponent that causes it to come about.

It need not be the result of periods of illuminate introspection, though in its best cause, this is certainly the most preferred of any other!

The process of continually shedding our past is a necessary destructive effect casting previous paradigms to the winds of self-understanding so that we may emerge into an all new paradigm of self-understanding in our present! Many names have been given to this very effect.

Holy intervention, karma, divination, Magick, evolution, and a host of other novel affectionate labels.

No matter the name given to an egg, an egg, is still an egg! What hatches from them all when they are allowed to nurture and then break apart destroying

their presence allows new life to emerge and to grow!
It is a fascinating postulate, EH?
In the Devil's way~!

Psychic Presence Creating Your Life!

Sometimes after a long nights foray beyond the veil, we awaken feeling as if we've connected and traversed a great spirited journey of some type! Sometimes we feel like we've spent time reviewing the past, spent a great time in contemplation and connecting with the present, and focused on our future.

The psychic connection we have with the reach and the intensity of our own spirit is beyond possible depiction. It moves beyond the stars themselves because we move beyond the stars themselves!

Suffice it to say that we have the capacity through the power and reach of our spirit, through our psychic potential to enact great present change through the construct of our own sense of personal revelation!

Remember to not lock yourself into a repetitiveness of what are the memories of past paths and old ways of being, in lieu of what you are meant to be moving towards today! This is why we review, so we may finally let go and move on!

You were never intended to reside in your past because there is no power there for you any longer.

The only psychic strength and power that is yours resides in the right here and now! This IS what truly determines your forward moving path!

Renewing Your Spirit!

You know, there is something about the presence of a slow rainy day on the ocean bay that sets a peaceful mood within me for some reason. The gulls are calling overhead as they gathering their breakfast. An occasional striper breaks the waters surface interrupting the rain rippled patterns and the accompanying sound of sailboats masts waving in the breeze adds to the call of the setting.

Every brand of day carries its benefits to our spirit both, cloudy or clear, sun and rain!

On days of grey and hanging haze, sometimes the best thing we can do for ourselves is to allow a little bit of a spirited recharge and a fulfilling renewal.

Take in the energy, the darkness and the light, and the calming effects of the cool rain coming off of the ocean. Allow the clouds and the scent of the salty air to reinvigorate your soul!

Do this for yourself wherever you are! If you're not by the sea and perhaps in the Midwest, the North, or in the mountains, choose your own special sort of site, spot, and setting to renew and recharge yourself!

Resting Your Lamb and Projecting Your LION!

A magnificent Monday morning and a wonderful week to you all my dear friends!

How you set about determining your attitude about yourself can determine a lot for the tone of your entire day, your week, your month, and even for a longer stretch of life! If we wake and scowl about all of things that we convince ourselves is wrong about us, that we're not attractive, we're not worthy, you now the scheme; then this is the way that we will project ourselves to the entire world around us!

Ever hear that old saying; "Fake it till you make it?"

None of it is telling us to fake our way through all of our life. What it's really telling us is to put out there before us how we truly envision ourselves as being, and not in how we might feel in some antecedent moment of time.

You might feel tired, grouchy, unworthy, unattractive, unresolved, unsuccessful etc., but if you draw out of you that powerhouse of a vision of the soul you "KNOW" yourself to be at your very core and then put this out ahead of you along your way, the world will stop seeing you as a mild mannered frightened kitten and instead will start to see you as that Grand Majestic LION that you really are!

Start today to project the true you that exists at your core, be damned to anything or anyone that would convince you of anything otherwise!

Shift Fear into Love! Into POWER!

There's a two-sided coin with power of each strong calling that draws you within, on one it endears and it's covered with fear and does taunt you to whittle no win. On the other is love sent from starlight above which does never betray or cut down, its strength is aligned with your spirit times nine it empowers and lifts you profound!

Now the fear side for sure it all filled with no more than its darkness and pain and its plight, it does tempt you to think that through hatred you'll sink all of those who you fear and who might!

As you turn it again and you shine love from then, that point you will always know true, that its power and strength does beat all other links that would try to destroy all that you knew.

So the choice is quite clear of the two you have here and the time for your choice has arrived, either fall to your lair drown in fear and despair and spend life on a path dark deprived.

Or side on the flip sailing like a tall ship steering far toward the light and the sun, shifting fear into love calling angels above to bestow of your grace that you've won!

Of this theme it's quite clear that the world is quite feared with tincture of darkness and ill, but a shift into love draws the powers above and does raise you right up like a spear!

Struggling To Achieve that True Power in Friendship!

Resentment and unnecessary anger serve nothing. They alter your consciousness to ill ends. They resolve only to keep you in a state of dark repute.

Eventually if allowed they can become a bad habit and you know what becomes of a bad habit if left unchanged? It evolves into a lifestyle! Do you really need this as your life?

I'll share this much on this subject.

In my past there were countless years where I would actually overextend myself, all my energy, and virtually any possible resource I could to the point of losing jobs and even exhausting myself financially in trying to figure how to build up what would only and usually prove to be lackluster friendships and pseudo-relationships in my life!

When I reached that point of literal exhaustion and emotional despair about my attempts to make all things work out no matter what between these so-called friends and myself, then it all finally dawned on me when I returned to a calm and true state of personal awareness!

I finally accepted that anyone out there who truly did want to be my friend and to be in my life would make an equal attempt to be there for me as I did for them. If someone doesn't want to be in your life, you'll know it!

Don't lie to yourself trying to disprove your own intuition! In the end it will only serve to dismantle your own sense of dignity and your inner peace!

Your true friends will always be there and yes, you will know who they are!

Those who leave you, never were in the first place.

You are worth better than that.

It serves nothing to struggle to achieve deeper bonds with those who will always view you as nothing more than a mere acquaintance.

Taking a Leap!

In order to determine where it is you are truly destined to go with your life, it usually helps to first set yourself about the task of "disciplining to listening!" To yourself that is!

Life tends to travel about in inches and specks when it comes to unveiling revelations! Sometimes though, it spans great chasms of realism like a leap across the universe and this is where we apply terms like "Quantum Leap" when these leaps reach beyond perception itself!

The thing to remember is that such a leap is created from within, is perceived from within, and is realized within! Everything from without that is added to the mix is just icing on the cake of life!

Tonight as you lay your head upon your bed, spend some time unlocking the doors of your awareness and begin to field the formula of that leap you've been waiting for! I have news! They never come from outside of us! They are always an inside job!

The Absolute Emerging in Our Lives!

Alas dearest ones, as this day has been won, and I set my sights now to the veil. I pray most do that you all so right through will be filled with great peace in your sail!

Most days are settled in wisdom and spice while footsteps take just a while longer, through whistling winds our patina roughs in and wrestles with deep thoughts thereafter. Now most do say that as we may make of our lives as demonstrated, we surely do fish for every single wish and make of the moat quite berated.

Once the dust has calmed and the light its charm and the sunset all rules the way, look forward we do for some peace what we knew would be most of our parable waved caster. But the trueness to life as surprising as ice down beneath on a warm summer eve, is that somehow life does, all work out as it thaws any cold frightful jeers we might feel!

No matter how hard, how rough, and/or how taxing the path of my life has been up until this very point in time as I write this to you all, the one thing that has always somehow existed as the undercurrent of my soul is that; at the end of the bend, I somehow know that I will always turn the corner and see something better emerge for me regardless of how much I've thought I screwed it all up!

This isn't surety, and it isn't confidence! It's the ABSOLUTE power we create and unleash in ourselves continuously emerging of our existence and it always has been!

It is yours!

The Eye Perceives but the Beginning of Reality!

A very grand and peaceful morning and a smooth and happy pass through your weekend dear souls!

The ancient Egyptians signaled the presence of the deity Ra through the representation of the decorated eye that adorned its temple walls!

One of the reasons that the eye was such a focus of their attention to one of their prime deified figures was no doubt due to the same reason we in our modern age say that; "the eye is the window to the soul!"

Our eyes perceive and sense, they articulate expression, they open the doorway to our experience and they communicate our intention, they also run a direct line to the spirit, and the ancient Egyptians knew this as so do we!

Have you ever noticed someone you don't quite trust and then those that you do? One of the first indicators just might have been in their eyes, yes?

We form our understanding and construct our cognitive foundation about life relating to our world through our eyes and we comprehend and discern what we think we see according to what we believe is reality! Truth is that reality is much more-vast than what we merely think we see, but also what we allow ourselves to see, to sense, and to perceive!

When you look into a mirror today, take some extra moments of time to explore your own eyes deeply! Scry a bit into them, and then openly and honestly let yourself feel and comprehend what you perceived within them!

The Greatest Personal Power Ends and Begins Again with the Tone of Your Spirit!

For me, there is little more peace evoking and infusing of the spirit of magnificent life than the energy of the dawning sun over an ocean bay!

Salem Bay is one of those places for me that hearken to my soul! It fills my spirit with a sense of wonder and happiness!

If you wish to set this tone for yourself in your life for your life every day, set a scene, a picture, a painting, or some place where you may meditate for even a minute or two every morning and don't let the thoughts or the intrusions of others offset or spoil your magnificent spirit of peace and strength!

But, don't mislead yourself as to the power you manifest at this center you seek and divine.

WE are the power of ultimate creation and this will always be so.

Spend a minute or two out of every day, then express your embracing of your own sense of personal power in a magnificent way!

The greatest power you can ever express begins with the tone of your own sense of spirit!

The Impact of Intimate Friends!

Regarding those who are your most intimate friends, those who believe in you especially when you find it difficult to believe in yourself!

I have benefited from having several such magnificent souls in my personal inner circle over the years! In times of trial they held me up. In times of despair they gave me hope.

In times of grief they feed life.

In times of anger they give peace, and in times of rage, they give hope.

In times they also draw away from us.

Pray that all would have one such soul in their lives as well, for when you do, appreciate them for what they are, and love them for what they add to your own life!

However, remain wise, and careful to and of whom you refer to as true and real friends.

For most will not be, and will never be, and this is the saddest truth of all.

The Magick that is Home!

My friend Marvin set the tone of this morning's thought for the day! It's amazing how much that place we always knew as "home" never truly leaves us no matter where we should ever go in our lives. I think one of the most eloquent quotes I've thus read to date on the subject of home was written by the screenwriter and filmmaker J. Michael Straczynski. He said that:

"Home isn't a place; it's where your passion takes you."

Home is all wrapped up in those places where we've painted the portraits of our memories. It's where we've lived, it's where we've loved, it's where we've celebrated, it's where we've struggled, and it's where we've grieved.

It's sewn into the grand complex tapestry of our lives and while some identify it with a house, an apartment, a neighborhood, or some other place that holds a warm spot for our soul, home really is what we always carry along with us of that place and of the family and the people who made it all that it was!

It's all of that which makes our lives feel all the more worth living with that special bit of passion that only "we" know means home in our hearts!

"Home.." really is "where your passion takes you!"

The thing to remember is that your passion for life is everything that makes each day all the more worth living with as much energy as you can insert into it!

Live today with your own special passion for life!

The Manifesting Magick of Our Imagination!

Alas my dearest ones, as we all ready ourselves for our nighttime's veil, we again move beyond worlds and construct the Methuselah of our own divination! Settle in your soul that all we could ever imagine for ourselves is but a glimmer of the reality that we have yet to unfold before us!

Magick it's been said is the propellant of the soul making itself manifest upon the world around us! If this is to be true, then perhaps we could say that all of what we could possibly imagine as being real in our lives, has only yet to be seen if not touched due to the nature of creation itself being the result of the power of one single grand manifesting thought!

Is life an illusion? If so, then as we stitch of this emerging tapestry of life, so do we color its threads according to the Magickal imagination we determine to make real in our lives!

The Momentary Darkness in Neighborhood America

In a time littered with darkness of expression, it's easy to begin to lose your perspective on the brighter scenes of the moments of life.

Nowadays we all seem to be constantly beleaguered with a constant river of tumult and viciousness of character, the audacious nature of which is difficult for anyone to even begin to contemplate in realistic perspectives let alone to try and accept as being real!

Between so many wars and actions of terrorism targeted in the name belief, with the current nationalist tensions that could rival some of the most confusing days of the late 1890's when most or all of Europe was literally an armed camp loaded with paranoia and all just awaiting that single spark that could ignite the worst of all their fears.

With the continuing presence of the unsteady foundation of local politics and economic fears creating an unsteady environment of unsure security as well as the revering of a "Mayberry" way of life seeming to be long since past our possibilities. On top of all of these and many more, we all sit and ponder if even in the most brief and silent of ways, why it is that those thankfully rare of individuals in our midst choose to do the things that they do?

One of the stanchions of hope and praise that we've always looked upon and that we've always had working in our favor was the image and the visage of the positivity residing in neighborhood America!

Why is it then that we again are witnessing the presence of such horrific and terrible events as we have seen unfold?

Well, certainly in psychiatric circles there will be many who will recite chapter and verse on standards and diagnoses both potential and historic. In locally political ways there will be the releases of supportive thought for their community.

In Policing terms from our brave and gallant men and women serving our communities there will be assurances relating to their hard work to see to our safety and our security. All very proper and all serving to help the rest of us to find a sense of soul between one another throughout all the tragedy!

Then there are still the core questions that will still remain regardless of all of the hope being expressed. The question will still remain.

"Why?"

Every household, on many sidewalks, in many coffee shops and in every church pew they will have their instincts regarding what it is that could move someone to act in such a dark way? Most will resolve themselves to the presence of a definite core of some form of illness that worked to promote such motions of being.

Then of course the questions and the grief will still remain after all has been said and displayed across television screens, in community gatherings and within newspaper headlines.

"Why?"

In modern neighborhood America how could such events still take place?

It goes without much stretch of thought to conclude that something went terribly wrong somewhere within the spirit of such thankfully rare souls in the world who choose such horrible ends in their lives.

In personal thought, for myself mind you as we all will come to our own conclusions, as I think on the places and the people I have come to call home and my special spots in my own parts of the world, I remember that at their core, there are some who by virtue of their own self vision and the evolving lacking in its clarity, there is somehow a loss of spirit that suddenly resides in such souls.

For some reason instead of steadying into a soulful spirit of some hope for the future, that life will indeed get better, and that feelings for what they are will all eventually pass dawning to brighter and better days yet to come; a few instead make horrible choices that lead to even more horrible ends.

We all recognize that many throughout all of our great communities work hard to reach out to one another to express that hope does exist and that nobody is ever all alone! The professional hands and the human hearts are present in all of our communities from all of the aforementioned and more to try and lend aid and support to those who for their own reasons may feel lost, alone, very scared, and understandably powerless in their lives!

Hey, let's face it! As John Wayne murmured to Katherine Hepburn in the 1974 Film Rooster Cogburn:

"Life's ain't an easy game sister…" Its not!

Life really can be difficult even in its brighter of times! Life can take hard and challenging turns as we try our best to move our ways beyond the fog and the battle smoke that seems to constantly emerge on our individual and our collective horizons.

It's a dark path that emerges at the point of making such tragic decisions as we have seen unfold in recent days.

There are no ideal ways of explaining any of them away or of settling the souls of the many millions standing at the sidelines in absolute awe of such tragedy.

The single-most quality that remains between us all is the steady hand of the hope of the spirit that we have between one another.

No, there are no words can take the pain away, there are no words can settle the fears or make adequate excuses to the children or to any of those older souls in our midst for that matter when they all ask that common single word;

"Why?"

For me I try to remember to seek out the hope that I see existing between everyone as we all try our collective bests to move forward. I try to remember that such dark paths are not residing around every corner of our neighborhoods. I try to cast a silent smile to my neighbor and to the people I pass on the street because that's the best I have to offer others as I walk by them on most days.

After all of the questions have been asked, after the grief has taken place, as all of the media have their moments, as the rest of our nation moves forward, I think what really remains is our individual sense of hope adding itself to the person right next to us that helps us all to move beyond the tragedy.

The spirit that remains between us all is that there are better days ahead and in them is the hand of support we all offer to one another!

The Only Loser is that One Who Chooses to Give Up!

If your anything like me, you've certainly made your fare share of err's along your way! Some fade to grey and depart like a sunset. Some are like "Nessie" occasionally popping up from time to time to remind you how fallible you are; and some yet still just seem to alter your path to whatsoever unknown ends. One of the mysterious things is that in some architecturally designed way for the soul, all of our errors somehow end up working for us along the path to our destiny!

Why? How? In what shaded way could it possibly all help us?

Don't try to answer all of these ponders, you'll end up with a spiritually induced ice-cream headache, believe me, I know!

What I can tell you is that many things happen in our lives through what has to be described as none other than "intentionally designed abhorrent chaos!"

The most amazing thing is that through all of this chaos that we wade our way through in our lives, the powers that be that act in our favor somehow make sure that a grand bit of design in it all always works for us!

The only loser in all of this is the one who chooses to GIVE UP, figuratively or ultimately, instead of continuing the path forward and letting things work out!

The Veil of the Moon

The nighttime's sail towards a moonlight rise on calm seas feeds the soul, just as the wise understand the wry in life feeds fears of old. To seek such peace as wrapped in fleece and solitary muse offers you, is found aboard that ship from shore so far away from unease. So as you review your daytime through and thoughts refuse to let go, just close your eyes and then surmise that ship sleekly cruising toward ore. Our souls as fixed within our nix are always seeking that light, even of the moon in nighttime's rune feeds well and calms our plight!

Think of your spirit exuding its brilliance from the seat of your soul as that of the sails of that ship moving calmly towards the veil of the nighttime moon!

Trials and Triumphs Towards Your Destiny!

Often you will ponder on the reasons for your day, for why it remains that many senseless reasons move your way. Often times you seek for perfect paths into your light, from struggles every morning leading on to very weary nights.

Often times you laud of those little things you find, and often times you're wary of the troubles you might mind. But most of all the greatest of all things you come to do, is to awaken to the path that leads to all that's meant for you!

No path that we choose to take is a wrong path! Some are more direct than others. Some wander and provide incredible yet challenging experiences. Some really are designed for the record books!

But, "ALL" paths lead toward our destined future! The thing to remember is that somewhere down the line, we will inevitably realize that it all was for a reason, those trials and triumphs that landed us right where we were always meant to be in the first place!

Trusting Our Intuition!

I saw a quote today that literally set off frequencies around me! When I get tuned energy like that, it's something that should be shared, so thus I do.

"Trust your first intuitive thought! It comes from your higher self which is connected to the whole!" – Awakening People

I can attest to this most heartily!

Whenever in the years of my life I have dispelled with my first intuition and passed it off as workings of only my imagination, these are the times I ALWAYS wished that I had. Now, I do not. PERIOD!

Do you know what the differences are between a seasoned Psychic and Medium and a Novice? Very little actually!

That is except for several core qualities that obviously vary between all people. These are the inherent traits of intensity in perception, allowing themselves to remain tuned when most others turn away, learning to be understanding of what they discern, and most critically, ABSOLUTELY trusting of their intuitions!

Unfolding Your Power Through Your Footsteps!

Alas my dearest ones! As you set your head down on your bed and ready yourself for bliss, allow your means their skylight beams and part the veil with this! You can't raise yourself up by assassinating the characters of those you hold resentments against! You can't achieve true success by veiling the accomplishments of others.

You can't help yourself to feel more at peace with yourself by making yourself so busy you won't have the time to attend to what's really going in inside of you, and, you won't discover your true path in life by always following in the footsteps of others as they move along their own.

Be a rebel! Walk down a path nobody has traveled before and find yourself there!

Use Your Time Wisely!

When the day ahead appears to be busy and full and time is especially well notched, and nothing can stand and remain unmanned to be done with a well meant watch. Just take a moment to try and recall with conscience of mind quite smiley, the less of time that you have on hand, the more you need to use it wisely!

Wax Your Life Devilishly Eloquent!

One of the things that we tend to overlook as we become betwixt by odd and sudden happenings and challenges along our way, is that for every problem there is also a solution!

"There are always possibilities!"

I remember when I was at University studying engineering. One of the common sense rules that was always understood was that for every engineer drafting his or her brilliant designs, there were ten technicians ready to fix and redesign those same creations!

A famous saying from various Christian Theologians of the world is that:

"God is perfect, Gods creation is not!"

Good talking points but horribly simplistic and all too demeaning.

What however do you think might happen if such a grey paradigm was in fact "the real" falsehood and what if all of creation was indeed perfect right from the beginning?

What if everything that we understand as imperfections in the vast tapestry of creation were actually manifestations of our own redesign?

As a means of sewing and re-stitching our own tapestry it just might be that we are crafting the living and creative body of our own universe and it just might be that we are the technicians of our own lives and our own world leaving the Gods standing aside watching all of creation unfold before them?

Here's a revelation!

Something tells me that there are indeed no imperfections in the entire universe! The only imperfections that exist reside in our own creative contemplations which we continuously are seeking to upgrade, to make different, to make better for ourselves and in it all, eventually, we're going to get it right!

KEEP ON REDESIGNING and WAXING YOUR WORLD ELOQUENT TODAY!!!

We Are ALL Masters!

How we envision ourselves, especially if set contrary to that which is the finest and the purest of truths in our own understanding about ourselves, sets the tone for the construction of our own "congruence", or, the alignment of ourselves to our own true manifested being!

"We are all Masters!"

Every single one of us has within ourselves the capacity to touch upon, to awaken to, and to alter the very essence of our being through the wisdom of the ages that lives and makes itself known within and through us! The thing that most bypass along their way is that they refuse to align themselves with the congruent symmetry that allows every fiber of their existence to vibrate at their greatest possible frequency!

As physics has alluded to; everything vibrates! Everything is manifested and made real through the energy that is constantly in a state of living action! Within each of us is the tuner that connects and strengthens our being to the greater whole that is the universe! To make it work for us, we must first recognize and accept the truth that "WE ARE ALL MASTERS!" Then after accepting this truth, we must swing open wide our doorway to LIVING IT and then sharing it with others!

When we truly wish to make the lives of others brighter and better through this grand revelation, we make better and brighter of ourselves through our magnanimity and the overall effect of this is that we work to bring our own collective whole into greater alignment with a more powerful self!

It sort of works like a great picture puzzle!

As we set each piece into its place and bring more energy into line with one another, we all become stronger, we become wiser, more intuitive, and yes, more powerful!

Remember the saying: "Knowledge isn't the beginning of wisdom, the lack of it is!" What this is really telling us all is that: "Awareness isn't the greatest strength we have gained at the end of our journey, it is the doorway through which we come to understand that we are ALL Masters at this!"

Wonder is the Ageless Spark of Wisdom!

When I was a boy I wondered on things, on marvelous lights, and great flying wings. I gazed upon heroes so storied and tall, and listened to music, from the stairs down the hall. As I grew I carried marvel of the things up in space, of the ghosts of the air, and the animals in their place. Then I grew even further and then wetted my mind, upon numbers and structures and then responsibility arrived!

Growing older I then pondered on the cause of it all, what brought about life, and what propelled all that's small. Even older my own life made me feel so confused, quite the thing of the fabric of a bit part eschewed.

Then in old age I realized all the things I had learned,
were the spout of the tip of all things yet to be heard.
Because suddenly I realized as my grey came of age, as
my skin loosened bits, and my joints ached parlayed.
For I then sat and pondered of the things I then knew,
was that wisdom come with wonder, and aware
always new.
Then I smiled and recounted on what started it all,
not the line on the page, or the forms on the wall.
So I wondered all again, upon so many things, on
marvelous lights, and great flying wings. I gazed upon
heroes so storied and tall and listened to music from
the stairs down the hall…
It's true you know, that wonder is the spark of
wisdom that ignites when we're young! The thing to
remember is that this never changes! WE CHOOSE
TO CHANGE WITH AGE!

You Do Have a Destiny!
Every night presents a passage to us in its own very
special mystic quality just as every dawning morning
we greet breaks through the veil of darkness leading
us to a brand new day filled with wonder and
opportunity!

Fill your hearts with the understanding that as you look out upon the world this day and yet again think on your emerging path, without exception understand, you are at the right moment, at the right time, at the right point in history, to do something positively magnificent for yourself and for the entire world!

All that is stopping you is your belief in yourself and of the powers that be that are with you!

Dispel of the little things that you've been dragging along with you so far! Throw away those irritants that have offset your conscious thoughts, those weights that have dimmed the creative Magick of your spirit!

You do have a destiny!

Now begin to fulfill it!

You're the Executive Producer!

Somewhere in the ether that is the backstage of the universe we all have a supporting crew that is arranging our makeup and our wardrobe! They are setting the brightness on the lights, adjusting the energy levels, and they are raising the contrast on all of the Magick that creates every moment of our day!

The one thing that we ourselves have carte' blanche control over, that we are the ABSOLUTE Executive Producers of is our script that is constantly evolving and changing in setting, style, decision, and every scene and moment as we constantly do our own script re-writes!

We have consultants, oh yes we do! The influences upon our evolving script are vast! It all comes from the Gods, the Goddess, our Guides, Our Angels, passed family and friends, passed pets, living family, friends, pets, acquaintances, and situations. Our living script is what commands the rest to emerge and where we go from there, is up to us!

The big question always remains: What will the next BIG episode introduce? It's all up to you! YOU'RE THE PRODUCER!!!

Your Greatest Adventure!

Sun sets my dearest ones, and with it the entrance to a new and revitalized vision of the darkness that makes life incredible and sends your spirit to its greatest adventure yet beyond the veil!

Cast a circle with a white candle and white sage to honor the purity of the spirits and your angels beckoning you to return yet again within the true realm!

Set forth your footstep beyond the light that construct of daytime living, emerge your spirit on through the veil and bring your soul along with it. With sage cast room with fern wind loom, then circle a clockwise wind, speak wish times three and then seek thee, beyond where spirits make nine!

Your Powerful Touch Alone Can Change the World! One of those many surreal things that we tend to lose our perspective of is that we are being watched over as we move about our day, even on the weekends! We're experiencing the presence of the ancients, of passed loved ones passed beyond the veil, and now returned back to visit us, we're experiencing the presence of angels, of Gods, of darkness and light. We are experiencing the Devil's Path. The path that leads to our ultimate illumination. This is the path concerned with our well-being, if we so choose. We're experiencing the presence of spirits, and most of all we're experiencing the presence of all that in our minds we accept as our understanding of the Gods! Even as we are our own Gods! With such a chorus of influence in our lives every day, how can we still convince ourselves that we weren't meant to persevere in this life?

Such is a choice, as failure and success.

Many question of what, in and amongst all of the current upset that is taking place, can there possibly be any good that they can do for others if not for the entire world? Well, it's all about collective strength and collective power gathered together to alter a world!

One person's touch can and does make an immense difference!

Your Special Magick is the Magick of Creation Itself!

Eventually in life you come to see that one day seems to just blend into another, and especially so throughout a busy work week! We begin on Monday and on into Tuesday, then into Wednesday and so forth while always keeping our eyes on "Friday" for our release from what seems to many like we're all in a constant effort at some surreal lifelong servitude! The reality that can spark a-light in our spirit, if we would allow ourselves to recognize it though, is that each day, every hour, every moment that we live is a constant thrust at infusing our experience of life with our own very special bit of Magick!

What we think, how we interact, all the problems we solve or try to in any given day, what we create, what we battle, what we succeed at, and most critically; "all of those we help along our way", is all an expression of the spark of a special brand of Magick that ONLY YOU can create as nobody else!

You doubt this you say?

Then look deep into the eyes of your child, your significant other, your parents, your sibling(s), your coworkers, your clients, look deeply into the eyes of the people you deal with on each of your days and then, DARE to look into your own eyes in the mirror at various points throughout your days! Try then to convince yourself that you're not special and that you're NOT a VERY SPECIAL spark of Magick in your own special way!

This is the sort of incredible revelation that so frightened those power broker's and the many religious and political leaders alike of so many Lands and Provinces in the Middle Ages! It's also why they set so many to the flame in those "Burning Times!" The hard fact is that the LAST THING that anyone with any tenuous grip on any sort of public power ever wants to face is for the people under them to come to the intimate understanding that they have an immense personal power within themselves to spark great and lasting change that is completely "uncontrollable" by those in so-called power!

Consciously expressing your own Magick is an act as natural as breathing which is why there are some in the world who fear its very invocation and would create an absolute battle against its brilliance and manifestation!

Your special bit of individual Magick is the Magick of creation itself, from within creation itself, formed in the consciousness of the source of creation itself! Now THAT is absolute M*A*G*I*C*K!!! LIVE IT!

Your Time Will Come to Shine!

One of the most profound and indelible living truths that we all are impacted by is that we all act as beacons for one another at some point or other along our way!

Have you ever heard the saying that "one person's teacher is another person's student?" Well, the aligning truth that also applies here is that "one person's bane is another person's beacon!"

We all shine in our own way one way or another. At some point it will be YOUR TIME TO SHINE and when this is, there will be a reason and a purpose for you to do so for the better good of others!

Your Wellspring of Creation!

We all seem to be what and who we all appear to be on our surface as far as most others in the world are concerned. Heck, many of us just take ourselves almost virtually for all of what we perceive as seen in our own mirrors every morning without seeking much more if anymore self-revelation along our way. Truth is that beneath our concrete outer shells we all have within us a great font of soulful potential just waiting to be drawn from like a refreshing well deep in the woods!

We all have at our avail a deep and soothing, a powerful, a strong, an endless and universal channel to the power that created us and everything that we perceive in our midst! It is through this source that we live, create, adapt, experience, challenge, and yes, occasionally fail only to reinvigorate our spirit then rising again to a state of achievement!

The worst mistake to ever make is to presume that as a rule of your existence you are all alone and that you have no power within yourself whereby you may shift and change, and adapt and create a new path with new experiences and new Magick at any point in your life!

Today, why not start believing that you may at any time draw upon your own well of creative Magickal strength and power?!

THINK, then BE, then ROCK ON!
Hold to your own in your magnificent way for as long
as your brilliance will have it, although in case you
run out of space there's always your spirit to expand
it. The thing to recall is that all in all the nature of the
world that is, is formed envisioned your soul casts in
it 3rd eye called forth from this.

Its easy do tell just like a spell though simpler in
terms implicit, your thoughts and dreams that form
your seams, the architect by which you'll win it! So
next you dream of life you've seen in mists of mind
and thought, uncaged your vine of spirit so fine the
power through which we spin it!

It really is true you know, that the literal magick of
the creation of all our experiences in life manifest
through that greatest creation engine that we all have
within us!

We T-H-I-N-K then we BE!

The trick is to truly recognize and accept that the
"THINKING" part is as much a means of promoting
our own existence when by following it up in the state
of "BEING!"

Although also recognizing and accepting that the
state of BEING is as real as our thoughts, is the crux
of the stalling point where many lose their steam!

Believe and then let it roll! Or as I like to say…:

ROCK ON!

We Are All a Transience!

I've heard it asked why it is that deeply insightful and greatly intuitive (psychic mediums) people tend to be loners where their greatest abilities are concerned? Not as people in a social or any anti-social sense, but rather where their work and the expression of their spirit is concerned! This defines it well as far as I'm concerned, at least in my own case.

Such a state thus gives me time to wonder, to search for the truth! The question always is: "what is the truth to the matter, and what precisely is that "matter" to which we seek some truth of?"

We are all a transient Magick you see, an illusion of frequency, a gathering of energy, the action of waves and form of will! The soul is the source and the spirit is the means that we manifest and act and adapt and thus, so does creation at our glance! It's amazing that it takes a child and their unstained perspective to see all of this clearer than any other in our midst!

The peace we experience in our lives is a direct result of the attitudes we set as our foundation for each day! If we constantly invite darkness and turmoil into our path only because it's what we are used to experiencing, it will continue.

If however, we set our minds and our spirits to remaining centered and calm, no matter who or what to the contrary, then this will be our passage.

Sooner or later we all come to realize that more often than not, it isn't others who determine how our lives will unfold, it is we who set the tone of each morning that begins our day!

What Drives Your Illumination?
When in consideration to the matters of the energy that truly "is" our life, it sometimes is so easy to dispel in the mind the age old rumor that we are nothing but energy and if we do not attend to our needs, we quickly will begin to degrade and thus flourish about as good as a withering twig on an ice cold December evening!
The usual fare of hearing such things as: "a good breakfast is the best meal of the day", and "pace yourself" and "many hands makes for light work" are only some of the energy centered statements that have become commonplace in our world. What is usually never heard are those more energy intimate statements surrounding the conservation of energy, or the intake of specific levels of energy and how these all really do add to the overall well being of our bodies, that of course allows our spirits to conduct themselves as we attempt to craft our own grand experiments called life!

It is just never really a centered discussion for most in the world. That is except for communities such as this!

Hence this is one of the reasons why the term "enlightened" and seeking to become ever more enlightened is tacked onto living as we all here in our communities try to do.

We seek to understand the spirit, and we seek to understand our souls.

We seek to gain greater insight into the meaning behind why we are here, and we seem to be amongst the many who delve into those ethereal matters of the occult and the bane and benefit of such a thing as real vampirism.

We seek our individual identities along and through our paths of personality and through the expressions of all of those personalities.

None of any of it is inapplicable to any of what we all in these communities seek as a means to better augment the essence of our lives and nor does any of it detract from who we seek to be in our favor.

You see, this spiritualist recently wrote a detailed article on the broad descriptive nature of Magick and is planning an interlocked series on how we affect those spirits that are around us, as much as those spirits, or better put, how all of these ghosts do truly affect us as well as we craft our paths?

In this, the mind started to wander with the following question:

In how you continue to seek to better define your own life, your own essence, and to get a better handle on precisely why you define yourself as you do; how much do you singularly define yourself and how much do you allow other people, other things, and other life and spiritual experiences to add to your own definition of you?

Think on tendencies adding to the construct of your being!

Think to how the realm of the ether of your being is not only determined by your own thoughts and your own choices, but to how you are a product of also what is always around us all in terms of people, things, and yes, of spirits if you will?

How does your own path of enlightenment unfold?

What is a Witch?

Regarding what is a Witch.

Many have approached this question from so many perspectives. Some relate it loosely as being many related forms of spiritual belief intimately connected with even more related natural sciences, others have related the path as being a spiritual journey led by a path of Godly influences.

I've been rather inclined to agree with the thoughts of Israel Regardie on the path of magic and the Witch and other such paths of belief. Wherein he related that:

"the path of magic and/or that of the witch was one amongst countless many that are all directly researchable as well as systematically provable over time" and as they all seem to align conveniently with certain systems of spiritual belief spanning well over multiple millennia, its usually a relief to outsiders that the accord with the practice of magic that stands as integral to the path of the witch is one that in the end, isn't really all that different than any other way of religious thought that seeks to draw forth shifts in states of being as a result of that belief.

To me a Witch is a spiritual soul, who is one intimately connected with the natural science of creation as well as seeking ever deeper enlightenment with that they see as being of God, the Gods, the Goddess, and any and every form of the same!

What Is It I Seek?
Without a doubt, three of the finest questions we can ever ponder are:
WHO AM I?
WHAT IS IT I SEEK?   And…

.

WHY AM I HERE?

If you dedicate serious time to answering these three for yourself, then the remainder of your life will make absolute sense!

Our Philosophy of life is a concept worth pondering!

What is it Like Being a Psychic Medium?

I was recently queried to describe what it was like being a Psychic Medium? The following image and its accompanying revelation then suddenly flashed into my mind!

The peak of the water in a spring fountain is always transient, the pool however to which it eventually gathers again and rests until expressed again is its real source of power and strength!

At a much younger age, quite the time when you just don't think all that much on such things, I remember being very aware of many deeper of things around me. I can recall being aware of all people and especially of their feelings. I can recall being aware of the feelings and the happenings of souls in my own family when they weren't in the same place, in the house, car, or wherever I happened to be at the time. Emotion was always one of the keystones that formed the archway of my feeling of the essence of life. To me it not only served to define the other person I found myself focusing all my thoughts, senses, and my perceptions upon, but also of course with regard to myself!

Feelings I've always thought were akin to someone's eye, they tell the state and the presence of the spirit shining of the soul! Feelings and emotion tell the state of presence, of the charge of their lives! Ironically it's also beyond the veil of death where I frequently tend to grapple onto "emotion" firsthand and thus thereafter follow with more details…

Even in terms of the places I see, the state of humankind that is present in those places and the perceptions of what we call a "time", there are always states of feeling associated with it all. This is why I refer to myself in assertive terms as being very empathic although never restricted to the same! I never make the mistake of limiting myself or my visions of life and being!

Even in long periods when I found myself struggling to "be normal" and to be sure, it could have been more proper to call it "appearing as", as it seemed that most others around me identified as being "normal"; none of it ever really washed. It always felt like faking it, and after many years of moving to and fore like a ship on the Atlantic, I recurrently and always ended up back at that place where I focused upon my unsheathed senses and my perceptions again.

When that momentous day arrived where I did just this all over again for the several thousandth time running along, but then also added in my root spiritual beliefs along with it, it was like integrating a fuel rod into a nuclear reactor!

Suddenly there was an alignment that took place and I felt powered and whole to be sure!

You see, to ask a person who believes themselves to be living a very happy and fulfilling life in whatever their state as they are, is allowing them to fulfill what they consider to be the fabric in their tapestry of their lives. They at that moment might well see themselves as being happy with it all, match point, love, and done!

To ask a VERY MUCH aware Psychic Medium to stave off their senses and their perceptions however is like asking some other soul to cut off a foot or a hand, perhaps to shut away one of their eyes and ears and then asking them to go on ahead and perform their daily tasks as if to live what they are told is a "normal life!" It just cannot be done and feel whole.

Being a Psychic Medium to another person who chooses to not or refuses to not perceive or understand it is a certain mystery. In spite of everything else, there will always remain that proverbial deck of cards that in their minds is shuffled and then dealt out with suits and images simply as they are.

Being a Psychic Medium to a Psychic Medium however is no shuffle at all. To me, it is another sense and a perception as any other that has been integrated, used, expressed, grown, honed, exhausted, and given rest and then used again just like any other sensation and perception. It is the ultimate of unions in soul, spirit, mind, body, and essence.

The self-aware Psychic Medium doesn't really know a life or an experience of life where it isn't present. This is because it was never not present! Just like hearing, seeing, smelling, the tactile senses, touching the floor with the feet and smelling the nighttime air!

The Psychic Medium uses and exercises their senses and their perceptions along with their use and their presence because they cannot, not use them!

When I hear, I sense through thought and spirit.

When I see, I sense through eye and mind.

When I feel and perceive emotion, I allow the sensation of states of being mad, sad, glad, and scared of person and yes, of ghost and spirit; and yes, there is a vast difference between these last two.

When I think on the future, I am given the mind to perceive and pursue what may and will be.

When I ponder on the past, I am allowed to invade the past experience of those who endured life.

When I expand my senses and perceptions and then take flight to another place, I seek to reach out with my spirit and ask my soul to project this ultimate strength and to encapsulate myself upon other people, other places, and upon incredible events.

I know well what some skeptics say about me and I well know what they think of me and I've come to the conclusion that I may change neither, so as Sir Anthony Hopkins has so well said, "I've decided that their feelings are none of my business! I am what I am and I do what I do."

I know very well what my family says about me, I do know and can only suppose what many strangers say about me, and to this I've become very comfortable in the settlement that they too will never change and why should I try?

I do know what those few close friends of mine say about me, and I even know what a very few of my closest friends say about me, and I know of their doubts and criticisms of my abilities. Over a lengthy period of my life I've learned that their love will always be of a substance that I will in some way remember and adore, but what they consider to be their truth, and what I consider to be MY OWN TRUTH, are of a completely different order, and very probably they will NEVER truly join in unison. I'm ok with that. I have to be now.

Overall I've arrived at the following…

I've received many arrows shot at me over my years for a hell of a lot of reasons. We all have in life. It is a part of life! For me however, some of these wounds were intensely deep. I have however over these years eventually picked out these arrows and tenderly helped my wounds to heal. I then decided to set out upon my path, yet again, where I know I'll receive even more arrows as my years go on.

I do know one thing however.

I go on because I must go on…

It's hard. There are days and times when it's damned hard. Then there are days when I'm reminded that it's a cherished calling in life, and one that serves well all I could ever ask for.

There is a greater truth to my being here, and to all of those I was always meant to serve.

That to me, is what being a Psychic Medium is all about!

Go ahead and share this if you so wish. In its entirety of course!

I'm just one amongst a vast family of many.

Allegiances

We all have our allies.

We all have our allegiances.

We have associates, acquaintances, and yes, we all have our friends as many or as few as these may be. We all have those souls we place our trust in because we find that we must, often times despite circumstance or rationality.

It's the way of life for us and this is never an easy way it's been said. The choices we make with regard to those people who surround us are so very often littered with shortsightedness and error and some of the biggest mistakes that we all can identify with is when we find ourselves having bared ourselves if even slightly with another who in the long run was not worthy of our trust to begin with. It's a pain that strikes to our core in many cases.

Then there are those few souls who over time assure our own sense of grand perspective that in all things there is indeed a sense of dignity to be discovered, to be cherished, to be honored.

Oh, perhaps early on we found ourselves convinced that we could place trust where we did. Then for some reason, we found that trust violated, cast away, and/or simply shown a cold shoulders edge as it was the victim of the erosion of convenience and of course the arbiter our own sudden perspicacity.

It's important in such times to allow ourselves to regroup, to re-center, and most of all to return to a state of self-confidence in our own capacity to trust ourselves again and then to still trust others regardless of our bad experiences.

You see, others, just as we, will choose their own allegiances and their own allies usually out of a sense of convenience to their egos and their immediate need, and due to a shift they have chosen along their path. We all are unfortunately viably vulnerable to this instinct. It goes with the territory of being human.

Quite simply,… sometimes we just make mistakes in the spirit of some souls.

We all have the capacity to make our informed and our instinctive choices and we will, just as others will make their own. It will make it all a lot easier on your nerves if you resolve yourself to the acceptance that if this negates an association, an ally, a friend, removing your awareness and your presence from a person, an image, some company of souls, then so be it. Simply say to yourself that the time has come for you to move on to other things.

Oh there will be those times when you gaze into your mirror and think to yourself:

"I really have made a bunged-up mess of things in life haven't I?"

Forgive yourself for your own short-sightedness, and then, move on…

Try to deeply understand that when we choose our allies and those who will become known as our friend, that this is a choice we make with the understanding that it is the way we have chosen, it resides on a level of our own understanding that frequently surpasses our own implicit understanding.

Sometimes we must just accept that at that time, it felt right to us.

Then again, as we all, I make my own choices for my allies, for my allegiances, based upon informed and thoughtful experience, but also based upon the illumination of my soul and the expressions of my spirit.

When I've made my choice to stand with someone else, regardless of the popularity and the lacking of popularity in this choice, and when I know at my core that this choice is right, and just, and true to my soul, that's it. I will always stand by my decision, and yes, I will let people walk out of my life as a result of that decision and yes, accordingly I will also turn and walk away.

That's usually when you know it's the right choice. That's when I know that it is the right thing for me to do.

When we learn to stand on our own two feet in such decisions, then we know that we have emerged beyond the ego and started serving our soul!

Never let any experience however keep you from keeping yourself open....again.

Why Does the Universe Work?

"Every living being is an engine geared to the wheelwork of the universe!" – Nikola Tesla
There are many forms of thought relating to the formation of being in the world, the adaptation of our life and the universe, and the vast energy of the fabric of endless and infinite conscious spirited dimension that makes it all possible.
There are innumerable ways that these are celebrated, venerated, and yes, deified. Included in all of this however is the reality that we directly have a functional influence onto what unfolds and what emerges all around us! Some lately refer to this as the "Law of Attraction", others throughout history have called it the will of the Gods and/or God.
In and amidst it all however are those who recognize this universal force of power, this unrelenting strength is that which they call Magick.
However, you choose to recognize it, also do remember that the same force through which all things that we see, and all of that which we have yet to even perceive was created, is the SAME force that permeates from the core of all of us!

It is the energy of creation, the energy of existence! We don't simply use, direct, or manipulate that force in creation which we call power. We have come to understand that we, ALL of we, "ARE POWER OF CREATION" existing in-tune with everything else in creation!

That which we would be, WE ARE, simply because of what we are!

This is the sole and singular reason why creation works!

Yes, it is the tune of the Gods, of God, of the Angels, and of the Stars and all the Heavens! It is OUR TUNE!

Why Magick?

I think it may be a good time for a little clarity regarding just what is meant when those such as myself use and apply the term "Magick?"

What is being referred to in its many general forms isn't the "Magic" that ends with a "c"; that showman flair of stage illusion, of mirrors, and of lights. In this case here you see the "Magick" ending with a "k", that walks the paths of ancient ways of believing that also conjoins the study and the applications into the science of nature with that of the spiritual paths of some way of believing!

Its not all that uncommon with many other forms of belief in the world at least in its spiritual tone. In but one other way however, wherein as many engage in some form of prayer, some way of spiritual alignment, as we practice certain and obscure observances, and as we embrace of our own ways of believing in the purity of our own soul and of the spirit in its connections to the vastness of that we see as creation, there are those who also make it their living path to study those connections of the spirit to that of the manifestations in the creative forces of all of that of the fabric of nature that surrounds us! Hence why the passage has become virtual definition in that:

"Magick is the study of the science of nature, and of the spirit!"

In my personal life I recently yet again found myself in the position of providing a generalized watered-down explanation as to the outward appearances of our many ways of believing to a soul who upon looking inwards through our paned looking-glass, I thought must surely stand in some degree of amazement at just what all of this must be about? One of the realities faced by many who follow some walk of an ancient way of belief, is that as the world seems to continue on the road of its discreet progression in so many ways, in so many other ethereal ways we do also seem to be moving ever onward, further away from definite levels of intimate connections to nature, of spirit, and those many other colors of so many older world ways. There's nothing moral in any of this statement. It's just a reality! While I personally retain no conflicting values that may work to separate between those progressions in the machinations of modern science and technology to those more ethereal constructs in the science of nature and the tone of the studies into the spirit, I also try to always remember that there are many more modern minded souls who might and indeed do.

When I personally speak in terms of "Magick", it dawns in a multi-verse of applications regarding the manifestations of all of life, of spirit, and of soul. Of the dawning and the emergence of nature, our physical being, and yes, of our spanning and infinite spiritual being!

Yes, I speak in terms of the creation of and the recognition of concrete reality, the adaptations of the nature of our present reality; but also in the adaptation of and the emergence of a new and dawning future, adaptable by anyone with the will and the patience to seek out and to understand both the ways of old, and those ways all but new!

So when you see me personally use the term, "MAGICK", also try to remember, that there is a lot of content and context falling within this term for me, if not for all who apply it to their understanding of life, spirit, of nature, and of being!

Its more than just a thought or a way of thinking, it's a way of BE-ING and for many, a way of BE-COMING!

Why Should We Even Dare to Leap Beyond Logic? Well, that's an interesting question that on the surface deserves a good answer! Problem is that we all have a different answer with in no way would ever serve to prove or to relate of it in any experientially intimate manner for any two of us lest between one another. Hence the long and winding road that has always existed between those two venues science and spirit!

You see, on the surface, what we perceive as reality appears to be strictly an analog venture in the endless mix of creation!

The deeper truth to it however is that there are just some aspects of being that we in the oddest of our ways acknowledge as existence that are at least currently beyond our capacity to measure, to document, to place upon the tables of logic, and to fete out to the satisfaction of science and reasoning. Some things will require that streak of our higher reasoning centers, our insight, our sense of intuition, and a plain and simple leap of some form of many ways of faith in order to absorb and construct within the corridors of our minds!

Then it remains the task of our soul to validate them in such ways as we are willing to then accept them in even the slightest of tomes!

We are all absolutely boundless sensing machines! We are the most complex and comprehensive supercomputers that have ever been put to tissue and neuron out of creations great pea soup recipe!

We harbor the sparks of creation at our core, and we move Earth, mountain, and heaven with our minds, all while walking the paths of creating events, coloring seasons of experience, and exerting expressions of spirit that extend far beyond what we see as our own skin! Once we move through the boundaries of our own understanding, then we can begin to grasp that which we just might begin to understand as, eternity!

And to think, this is all contained along just the very first steps of what lie ahead for us all!

Logic presents some sense of rationality in the maelstrom that we perceive as creation.

Spirit is the extra-rational means through which we move our perceptions outside of the realm of logic and into the realm of the soul! One doesn't necessarily have to negate the means by which the other is expressed and understood!

Where Newton at one time searched for a reason that would explain why the apple fell, he also however spent great time seeking out the perceptiveness of his soul that gave the apple and its movement meaning in its existence!

Why?

Because Newton understood if at the least, that without a sense of meaning to the expression of creation, there was no reason for the apple to be present to begin with and for its own purpose!

Why Should We Dare to Leap Beyond Logic? Because logic surely serves, but that which leaps beyond it deserves!

When we seek to sense and to extend meaning and a sense of purpose and being to the grand existentialism that is our path of life, we may then seek out all of the logic and the empiricism we wish right along with it to try and help us to set deeper understandings.

Nothing in any form of logic however can ever or may ever take away or degrade the color or the quality of the tread that weaves that tapestry of life as a result of seeking to know and to understand the right dimensions of the thread that served to create it to begin with!

Logic only serves that which moves beyond it while that which moves beyond it may just serve logic better and to a greater degree than could have ever been true without that leap in the first place!

To take a leap beyond logic fulfills meaning and colors a sense of purpose while logic itself lays the stepping stones that gave that purpose a means to be in the first place!

You cannot truly have the aspirations of one without some sense of the other!

Is There Benefit in Daring to Be Different?

Why dare to leap beyond popularity?

Well, it really all sifts down to gaining your greatest strength in the genuine.

Da Vinci once stated: "Beyond a doubt, truth bears the same relation to falsehood as light to darkness."

There is no greater expression of a sense of spirit than that gained by walking what we each consider to be our true path although as importantly, genuine!

Everyone is different!

Everyone has a different color to the calling of their spirit! Everyone a different desire to the yearning of their wants, to their needs, to their passions, and of their own dreams in this life. As a result, we all find our own vision, our own journey, in our own way, and such an infinite color in the wide spectrum of the soul can never be well served through any one or mere numbers of tradition.

It's a bold assertion yet one that deems true in that as life colludes and divests of itself in infinite ways, so is the fabric of belief, magick, and of spirit!

Hence, there is no one way of life, no one way of belief, and no one way in the art of magick and if you will, creation!

And hence…

BE DIFFERENT!

This is the path that reaps ultimate power.

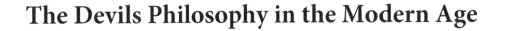

The Devils Philosophy in the Modern Age

Misconceptions, misconceptions. The fabric of these have caused division. The fabric of these have ignited feuds between families and the best of friends. The fabric of these have ignited world wars. There is no mixing any complex philosophies about it. The nature of that thing we call "misconceptions" have served to adapt and warp the very threads of reality itself, and often times in such a way so as to skew things so far out of proportion, that they've even caused deaths beyond number.

Think of the advent of happenings that brought about the period of time that we all acknowledge as the middle ages, and the dark ages in humankind's history.

Major powers of religion and misconception coupled with environmental factors and extremism of the most glaring types were the catalysts for thrusting humankind into a prolonged state of a deadness to its own possible ascendance.

Its been said that if it weren't for that period we conveniently call the dark ages, humankind today would very likely find itself exploring the stars instead of arguing with itself about the color and style of headwear and whether or not to continue killing one another over ludicrous belief systems that have done little else than to minimalize its own recognition of its own greatness.

Today humankind stands at a crossroads, the likes of which it has never before found itself. The major question is no longer:

"will we wake up to ourselves?"

The major question now is:

"how many will choose the path of their own awakening, and how many will remain clogging their ways through life acting like cavemen pulling at their own hair?"

These are the sorts of considerations that are driving philosophical minds now. No, Da Vinci is no longer with us. Yet, today we have a profound presence of so many of Da Vinci's ilk, and that's what makes the difference now.

Today humankind is engaged in a new age renaissance regardless of how many would rather the alternate.

One such misconception that some are grappling with now in this new age realm of humankind's own ascendance is related to the way that humankind is starting to recognize the old time religions and drawing themselves out of the darkness of their own own zombie-like irrational fears.

In the past humankind had the catholic church among many others who acted to control the very daily activities of a populace that had experienced plague, death, the very wiping out of a third of the worlds populations through uncontrolled illness and disease. The catholic establishment as many others grappled with ancient and very obsolete ways of handing out what they believed was their own labyrinth of rules and regulations for life that they truly thought would keep people under control and coming back to pay their weekly if not their daily penances to a church they were convinced was the only ticket into heaven.

Now, everything is different.

Humankind in ever-increasing numbers is no longer buying into the façade of idiocy that is the manner of an ancient religious rule-ness to the nature of daily life. No longer will a large portion of the worlds fabric of society buy into the idea that only some chosen souls ascend to heaven while all of the others remain crap out of luck.

Welcome to the awakening everyone!

Welcome to illumination!

Today the world perceives much of the old world religious ideology in a vastly different way.

Today humankind, much of it, has finally chosen varying paths of waking up instead of remaining in a half-dead state of slumber.

God is awakening to the conscious nature of people's minds and thoughts. The ancient Gods have awakened in the same way to the tips of the consciousnesses of humankind.

So too have the Angels returned, and this time they are not going back anywhere. They have now returned to stay!

This as witnessed by their presence in everyday life in just about any and every setting from the local coffee shop to the very poster boards of your local churches. Not too long ago there were rather poor attempts to try and paint a new rising color to the tinge of the wings of one of these beings we refer to as "The Angelic". That angels name humankind was told was "Lucifer", "Satan", The Prince of Darkness. Once heralded as the favorite angel who stood at the right hand of God.

Now, if we were to remain hidden in the middle ages, humankind would remain sure that Lucifer, or as we more commonly refer to him, "The Devil"; was always and will always be the personification of all that is evil. All that is darkness. All that is anti-life, anti-good about that which we all still loosely call creation.

Suppose this however.

Suppose that all of the ancient outmoded hyperbole of theology and words of the old world religious establishments were wrong?

What if all of this was the result of a few power-mad possibly crazy old men with inferiority complexes tithing down their own dark minded fear-based attempts at creating a being that hid behind every tree branch, hunkered down in every shadow, waiting patiently to tear humankind apart at the seams?

It all begins to sound like the subtext of some Hollywood screen play doesn't it? Surely it would make for a good movie! Oh yes, it has!

Here is the vexing problem. People long ago bought into it. They were handed a being that they were told was responsible for all of their ills, all of their sickness, all of their unexplained deaths, all the worlds wars, all the misgivings about even their own bad decision making on a daily level.

The Devil was handed to them as a convenient scapegoat, and now, is the time to set the record straight.

The Devil is seeking to clear his name for the rest of time.

Today at these cross roads where we stand is a facing rising dawn of awakening and many are looking onward, not backwards any longer and the Archangel the Devil knows it.

Michael knows it. As does also Gabriel, Raphael, and the rest of the chorus of the angelic, and that which you might refer to as the company of heaven. They have been instructed to move forward and to release humankind from its own passages of foolishness.

The spirit behind all of this is whom you ask?

Really?

Look within yourself. Seek within for the instincts to feel, and they will tell you.

Yes. God is behind all of this.

Oh yes, as with all ages of the past there will almost certainly relate such thoughts to the ridiculous nature of that which they call heretical talk. So be it…

Those seeking more, those seeking their own awakening will not, and it is those souls who will change every-thing and this is as its supposed to be.

Just who is the Devil, and just what is the Devils philosophy now in the modern age?

Well, let's just say that fire and brimstone haven't even the slightest scent to do with any of it. Hence the relation to why some will just resist even thinking of such things.

Irrational fears.

What if you were to be told that the Devil was not a fallen angel, and in fact, that there never was such a thing as a "fallen angel?"

Oh yes dark entities are a reality in existence, but that is another subject for another time.

What if you were told that the Devil in fact was, and still is at the right hand of the grand-maker, at the hand of God?

What if you were told that Michael never drove the Devil anywhere with his sword but in fact was and is the Devil's closest friend and ally?

What if you were told that the personification of that angel known as "Lucifer", "Satan", or "The Devil" was truly in fact a bearer of light and illumination, and that he has been moved to finally shift humankind into a new state and level of its own being?

What if you were told that the Devil was told to hand over the keys to the awakening and the illumination of humankind, to humankind at last?

Now, there would be a philosophy and a state of the affairs of being that certain religious elements would loathe at the very thought?

Well, humankind...

This is in fact the state of the grand nature to the spiritual affairs of humankind and now, everyone is being invited to finally step-up to their own awakening.

The Devil's philosophy in the new age is simple, yet as vexing and troublesome as it ever was.

The Devil's philosophy is rooted and nested in the path of two major things.

One, is "Awakening".

Two, is "Ultimate and an unrestrained Illumination".

All of it really is that simple.

Here is the problem.

If you tell a person that they have an open pathway to better-ness, to a greater state of their own ascendance and presence in creation, most won't believe it, and most won't even want to believe it. You see, people by their nature tend to be resistant to anything that breaks with their own facades of life, with their own paradigms that they have grown comfortable with.

Yes, we just got done saying previously that there is a new breed of humankind who was ready for its own awakening and its own illumination. Without a doubt this is indeed true and fact.

What abut percentages though? How many people are we talking about?

50%?

25%?

10%?

How about .05%?

If you chose the last of these, you would most likely be closer to the truth of the matter.

Yes, its less than even one percent of humankind would choose willingly to rise up and shed the skins of yesterdays ilk rather than not embrace its own ascendance.

Why then?

Why would the Devil, and the rest of the chorus of the angelic seek such a way if so few would embrace it? Well, for one thing, its because there is a force of ultimate spirit driving the pathway of this coming ascendance and whether people or angel alike like it or not, its coming, its happening, and it will happen. For this is the nature of all kinds of renaissance.

You see, there is a funny little habit that humankind has at its core that it just can't resist. Its sort of like the old British habit of standing in a Queue just to find out just why the hell everyone else is standing in that same queue? People HAVE to find out! People by their very nature are curious and they have to solve a mystery?

Here, the mystery is the very core of creation and being itself!

Now there is a mystery that everyone will catch on to eventually and the Devil's task is to carry this onward regardless of the naysayers!

The reasoning behind this is simple. Creation itself knows that the nexus habit is a true one. When one person of any sort of an illuminated nature tends to take a turn down an unknown road, the instinctive habit is that a whole mass of others will tend to turn in the same direction regardless because they HAVE TO KNOW!

"You doubt this," the Devil asks?

What then of Jesus?

Here was a man, he was a good man, a man of words and deed, who was put to death for his efforts. This one many, who simply talked and engaged in certain twists and turns to the path of thought and creation ended up being in at the least a part the nexus to the decline and eventual shifting of the entire Roman Empire, the then most powerful state on what was old Earth.

Today, the state-of-affairs is much different.

No longer is there a mount to hold sermon upon. Now all that is required is the presentation of the energy of change and illumination itself to take hold. In media. In text. In document. In words that carry the creative energy of change upon the very dawning to humankind's own level of consciousness.

This is the task at hand now, and as the Devil has faced an almost ageless period of humankind's own ridiculousness, the angelic though never give up. Their very job is to never give up!

So,…

What does the Devil say regarding his philosophy now in this, a new and modern age?

"Come. Come, and cast away the chains of your own imprisonment. Come and open your souls to the truth that is your own reality, your own existence as it was always meant to be. Release yourselves and awaken to what you truly are. For these are the words of God that I have been instructed to lay before you. Come and be. Finally."

What is the Devil's philosophy in the modern age?

Well, it isn't suffering. It isn't torture. It isn't lying, cheating, bidding darkness, demons, and all brands of ill to befall humankind as everyone has been told since the earliest days of the old worlds religious establishments.

What it is, is….,

Certain enlightenment.

What is the end goal you may ask?

That is simple to answer.

The ultimate illumination and ascendance of humankind to a state of divination, of its own self-divination. The ultimate ascendance to the level of that, which in your own way, in your own names, you refer to as being Godly.

" Do not believe in the traditions just because they are valid for many years in many countries. He does not believe in something just because many people repeat it constantly. He accepts something just because someone else has said it because it is based on the authority of a wise man or because it is written in the holy scriptures. He does not believe in anything just because it seems likely. Do not believe in the fantasies and visions that you think were given by God. He does not believe in one thing for the simple fact that behind that is the authority of a teacher or priest. Believe in what you perceived to be right after a long personal examination, in what is right for your own good and for the good of others. "
GAUTAMA BUDDHA

– Intention Ritual

Find a quiet place, where nobody can disturb you and Light a candle. If you like incense or have any other objects that are special for you, you can get them close.

On a small piece of paper, write your intention. Do you want awakening and illumination? Do a short meditation invoking your divine force who protect you.

We give you an example:

"I (your name), ask the divine force for aid in my path … (name your desire). I intend to complete this work successfully within one year and become ……. (write what you want to become). I ask to be open to all experiences and understand all lessons given to me. I ask to be accepted by spiritual guides and divine forces. So, it is."

Invite your spiritual guides to come into your life and read again your statement. Roll the paper like a scroll and tie it with a black thread, binding it and sealing your intention.

Keep the paper in a special place (on your altar) and don`t lose it! Sometimes, when you feel, light candles for God to help you in your path.

The Devil`s Invocation

" I invoke, The Bornless One, the closest Angel to the humanity. Thou art Man made perfect, whom no man has seen at any time. This is He whom the winds fear. Hear me, and make all my desires become true, so that I can change my life and my destiny.
I am He, the Bornless Spirit, powerful, strong, and shining like the immortal fire. I am He, the Truth, that lightened and thundereth and the Peace who can make all possible. I am He the begetter and manifester unto the Light and Darkness!"

Sins and mistakes

People need to be in constant communication with the divine, to spiritually evolve, to heal and to change their simple mortal condition. Recognition of sins and mistakes is the first step in forgiveness and correction. If you have fallen, do not be scared and discouraged, get up straight away and become much stronger. You will always be given as much as you can face it!

You will feel free from a burden recognizing the mistakes you made by writing a sheet of paper or talking with one of the priests. Recognition of sins is not a shame! The devil is the one who listens to people's sins and frees them to evolve and learn from their mistakes. It is said that the angels waiting for the souls at the gates between life and death will make your soul move easier if at that time you have the sins cleansed and forgiven during your life.

Short prayer for the forgiveness of sins

I ask for forgiveness of God for all that I have wrongfully or unwillingly done. I seek the enlightenment and awakening of the divine power within me, and I thoroughly study my feelings and deeds that I do day by day. I have to be closer to God, my creator, to be in constant communion with him to feel my soul how to get rid of any negative energy. Today I love, love and i love because I am looking for happiness and peace. The welfare of others no longer awakens envy and jealousy to my soul, and on the contrary, I feel joy and gratitude. My belief is every day that passes ever stronger, closer to enlightenment, and I began to believe in my powers. He wants my soul to be immortal, but I must to prepare myself for the next trip in peace, love, and happiness.

I'm proud of me, I love my life, I love my body and I treasure my immortal divine soul!

I want to rise above those around me who have chosen to live in a normality imposed by society. I want to be better, to vibrate love and joy and to help others find their inner happiness. I'm strong and I can make my dreams come true! I seek to learn from my mistakes and sins. I look around and see how people ruin themselves by accepting to live in hate and depression. It is your choice to help them arise or to step back and laugh! I am proud, and I see how every day I become my own idol. If I bring love to those around me, my life is right and pure.

I refuse bow my head to the ground in front of anyone. I am proud, fearless, I have faith in my own forces, I am in direct communion with God and I want to arise and shine!

The Devil`s Rules

1. Do not kill
2. Commune with God
3. Honor your family
4. Do not steal
5. You have no right over other people
6. I do not accept lies and false testimonies
7. We do not accept hatred and envy
8. Do not judge others
9. Give food to the hungry
10. Give water to the thirsty
11. Give clothes to the poor
12. Help the sick people
13. Do not turn the back of the one looking for your help
14. Bury the dead
15. Correct those who are wrong
16. Teach those who seek learning
17. Give advice to those who ask for it
18. Pray for your family and friends
19. Be patient
20. Forgive those who are wrong by helping them to distance themselves from their wrongs

Spiritual Bathing – Clean your energy and the body!

Millions of people take a sea bath, river bath or some form of spiritual bath every single day. In Africa, India, Americas, Asia and Europe, many rituals and ceremonies are conducted at sacred rivers and by the sea edge. Indigenous Gods and Ancestors are often honoured during these events and it is understood that their energies can help those bath in these waters. In colder countries people have an innate understanding that being by the sea or walking/playing within it has some unknown therapeutic powers. As soon as they see the Sun, people flock to the sea.

Water is a living intelligence, it has the most powerful magnetic abilities in the material world it is the only thing that can be broken up into minute steam particles, travel in the air and reconstruct itself back to the original state in another location.

As everything has been born out of water, the medium has the ability to communicate and hold all the energies on this planet, visible and invisible. Water is older than the earth and can never be destroyed; Air is just a rarefied version of water, basically a less dense form.

Spiritual baths, many just have hot bath with sea salts, sweet smelling oils, candles lit by the side and some soft music in the back ground. They feel rejuvenated and relaxed; they could regard this as spiritual as they feel uplifted and rested.

These baths may leave you feeling fresh and clean, however, unfortunately soap does not clean of energy. Across each day, you interact with many energy fields, some generated from negative/depressed people and other in less positive environments. These energies attach to your own like an unwanted guest. They can create a state of tiredness, unknown irritation, and sudden nervousness and sometimes just damn bad luck. We walk around asking why when we are not appreciating we can catch a bad mood, the same way we can catch a cold, by breathing in someone`s funky energy.

Cleansing yourself spiritually should be considered a daily practice. If only we all lived by the sea. For the rest of us, more deliberate measures are needed and in honesty, unless you know how to activate the deeper more powerful energies in the sacred waters, not all the attachments around you are removed. Please understand you have a very powerful life force, it sustains your bodily functions, your mind activity and generates a state of mind energy field, things like confidence, anger, joy and excitement, can be felt by others.

Energies and sometimes other people, want to live off that life force, which can bring a state of confusion and inactivity within yourself. As you try and muster energy to complete your own tasks, your mind is thinking of people`s issues or unable to focus on your situations.

Energies are trying to lower your frequency so they can sink deeper into you conscious to ensure their survival.

The spiritual bath will enable you to begin dislodging, agitating and eventually removing these attached energies. The problem is that you need energy to remove energy. The bath requires elements with life force to penetrate into your energy to where this unwanted guest may be located.

Your energy field is more like a place than a thing. Energies like to hide in different thoughts, feelings and memories. The bath should calm you down as energies pushing certain emotions should be removed.

Too many baths, too many herbs and flowers could be mentioned, this I fear could create confusion to the first timer. Those initiated and those with experience will hopefully know what works for them. I will only say in my experience no toxic items bleach, ammonia are not for me.

A white flower bath is good place to start. You can do it yourself and can expand when the general concepts are understood. This bath is the start not the end of your journey, not all your problems can solved in one bath. As your energy field clears up, your innate intelligence will start to assert more control over your thoughts and deny other thoughts from taking control over you.

White Chrysanthemum, Florida water, spiritual oil (if you have), a Candle, clean clothes and a sincere prayer. This is a basic foundation, you can add as you know or feel. The prayer is the real power key

Bath water added to 2/3 of the height of the tub. Break petals from the flower to the point where the surface of the bath water is covered. Add the Florida water 1/3 of the bottle, add you spiritual oil (merely prayed over oil) and whatever you may feel you need. Light the candle, compose yourself and ask the Ancestors to come to you help.

You can call on whatever energies you trust. I trust my Ancestors and in this bath I would call the Orisha Obatala , the Chief of the white cloth to come to help me remove the energies. Please call on those you are comfortable with, it will work the same .

Ask them to remove any energy that has attached to you and may be hindering your progress . Ask them to find the energies where ever they are hiding, leave no stone go unturned in their pursuit and do not listen to their stories for mercy.

Thank the water for holding the power of the petals life force, thank the flower for its petals and the energy they have given to your cause, thank the other items for their contribution to your progress.

Leave the candle to burn and the bath to set. The energy of your words has charge the bath. Your prayer intentions with diffuse into every molecule of the bath water making sure your life force and that of elements of bath can be used by the energies you have called via the candle to aid you.

After a least hour your can enter the bath. The room should be ready. Relax in the bath and think of the energies you called and thank them for the help they are giving you. If you feel the urge to open your mouth, let it happen as this is a sign that the unwanted energies are leaving.

As you raise your frequency, lower energies cannot live with you anymore.

Put on fresh clothes as your energy has now been cleansed and different from that before the bath.

Relax, try not to think of anything to heavy for the rest of the night.

This is a very basic bath to start off, there is a whole science behind using different herbs and items to create different affects for other situations. These baths are designed to clear the way so your natural intelligence can break through your fears and concerns. We have answers within ourselves, unfortunately we are sometimes just too afraid to ask the real questions.

This is like you baptising yourself into your own religion. Even though you have asked for help to cleanse yourself, you are still free and now not a slave to that energy. You are an energy asking another energy being to help you out. You have forgotten who you are and your real relationships with these energies.

You are powerful , you are the creator of the world you see in your mind, and your ego will try and convince you that you do not need this as you are alright.

The ego is an entity that has convinced everyone it does not exist. That one will be dealt with another time.

Good luck too one and all, this is just the tip of the iceberg, every journey start from the first step. Walk with confidence as they need you as you have the power.

- Spiritually cleaning your living space.

When you are out and about you pick up a lot of energies from the places you go to and the people you interact with or pass in your daily journey. A lot of that energy is negative and detrimental to you physically and spiritually. You can also pick up negative energy from people who are working magickally against you or in places that you move into that may have a questionable past and so harbor negative energies. Sometimes smudging is just not enough. That is why it is important that you as a Witch or Sorcerer set up your home as a magickal sanctuary and fortress against forces that would try to harm you or drag you down. There is a specific way that you spiritually clean your home. The first thing you do is to clean it physically. Get rid of clutter as much as possible.

When you clean a home, you should work from back to front. Take a clean bucket of water and add a handful of sea salt to it. Stir the bucket of water with your hand as you chant this charm: Water and Salt where you are cast no adverse spell nor purpose last. Not in complete accord with me. As by my Will So mote it be!! As you do this see the water in your mind's eye blazing with blue-white light. This water will now be charged to dispel negative/ evil/ imbalanced forces. You may now add a bottle of spirits of ammonia that you may be able to get from the pharmacy or barring that, household ammonia will also work (not the lemon scented variety folks) With household ammonia you don't need to add a whole bottle. a cup and a half should do. Prior to all of this you should have already swept or vacuumed your home from back to front. If you vacuumed, remove the bag, and dispose of it outside of your house. if you have a lot of floor space to be mopped begin doing that from the back of your home or apt to the front. Those areas that cannot be mopped like carpeted areas you can fill a spray bottle with the charged solution and spray. Get inside closets and behind the refrigerator and stove. open all cabinets in the kitchen and turn all glasses and cups drinking side down.

Put a large pot of water on the stove to slowly boil as you go through the house mopping and spraying. When you are done with this part of the cleansing, dispose of your bucket of mop water by either throwing it in the streets or flushing it down the toilet. Now is the time to smudge. When you smudge you are firstly using sage alone. Never blend sage with lavender or sweetgrass or other herbs. Sage does very well on its own. If you do not have sage, then dragon's blood resin burned on charcoal will do the trick as well. Smudge from back to front because you are getting rid of energies. Smudge all open cabinets and closets. Take your smudge to the front door of where you live and place it outside or if you live in an apt then place it on the window ledge and leave the window open to let out the smoke. Go get your pot of boiling water and throw it out of the front door with the intention of getting rid of all negativity and heated imbalanced energies that cause strife and problems in the home. Come back in the home, next you are going to need a fireproof skillet or pot. You are going to pour part of a bottle of either over proof liquor like Ever-Clear or 100 proof vodka or barring potable alcohol you will use rubbing alcohol.Place your hands over the alcohol and charge it with this charm: Creature of Fire, this charge I lay. No phantom in thy presence stay Not in complete accord with me, As I Will, so mote it be!!

See the alcohol blaze with blue-white flame and ignite it. Carry the flaming liquid from the back to the front of the house, visualizing a firestorm going before you cleansing everything in its purifying flames. Take this to the front of the house and let it burn out. Please be careful and do not set your home on fire. This procedure can be done safely. I have done it many times and lived to tell the tale lol. Now the final part. Rinse out your spray bottle thoroughly and fill it with a mixture of cool water, rose water or some other perfume like Florida water or Lavender water and a 1/4 tsp of sugar. Not enough to make a stickiness, just to reinforce the thought of sweetening the atmosphere in your house. Also make an incense of frankincense, dried orange peels and powdered cinnamon and light it. with spray bottle in one hand and burning incense in the other go through your home and refresh it from front to back. Keep the intention of filling your home with beneficial energies. Once you have finished all of this then you can proceed to the spiritual bath section of this post. The Bath should be done after you cleanse the house because the negative energies will still stick to you and you want to get rid of all of it. So, go straight to the bathroom and begin your bath. After your bath take three eggs and pass them over your entire body so they can pick up whatever residue is left.

Put the eggs in a paper bag and take a walk with them disposing of them discreetly. Make sure you throw the bag somewhere hard enough to break them and then return home by a different route. Now after you have done this whole ritual cleansing you will need to ward your living space against negative energies, magicks against you and things that go bump in the night that do not belong to you.

Prayers

I call the guardian angel
which God has given me
always be with me
to lead me into this life!
Awaken me, I am a God!
help me have money and success,
to be healthy and to help my family.
Move along with me, Always
and protect me from anything or anyone who wants
me harm!
I am Protected!

2. Prayer for travelers

I invoke my protectors now
to put around me the light through which no evil or
danger can pass!
* Feel how a glowing silver light begins to surround
you *
I'm protected and safe - say it 3 times.

3. Praying against disease

I pray to God, who can heal any disease of the body and soul,
Please God, say above me your magic words: "My body is perfectly healthy"
Name the affected organ, for example "My heart is perfectly healthy!" Say these words 9 times each evening for 9 days.

4. Prayer against trouble and anguish
Lord, I have dark clouds around me, and sadness does not give me peace. I suffer but I know you will help me to overcome this moment. * Light a candle *
You are the one who can send me my problem solving
* Name the problems *
Lord, I ask you to surround me with love and happiness and give me the power to go over this black day.

5. I am love and happiness

Every day when I wake up and go to sleep
When I cry and when I laugh.
My heart is clean, and I can see God inside my soul
I am one of God's children because I bring peace around me!

6. Prayer for marriage

My Lord, bless this marriage, you who care for all the human`s customs, you who created man by your likeness and made him master over his life and you said: "It is not good for man either alone on earth, so I will give them a pair. "
Unite our thoughts, souls, and hearts into one, eternal love!

7. Prayer for the dead

My Lord, take care of the souls of all those who have been close to me * say their names*, forgive their sins and mistakes and guide them on the right path! You are our creator and you decide our fate during and after life. Help me get over the pain that's in my heart now. Put around me your healing light!

Talk with me! Don`t judge but feel with your heart!

Day 1

Open your eyes and look at me
I'm part of your soul
Master over heaven and earth.
The sun is my crown, and the moon is my devoted sword.
I received you under my wreckage
and I anointed you with the palms of my hands.
I have given you the power to understand and to know me, that just by knowing me you will come to know the illumination.
But you, you lifted your voices and the swords against me.
When you understand that the balance of all things is me, then, I will turn my gaze back to you.
Step forward and discover yourself!
Open the gates of creation and truth!
Receive me with friendship, because I serve the same purpose as you!

Day 2

Can I hear your voices full of wonder, oh, my sons and my daughters, are you afraid of the flares of hell? Then look no further at the sun!

I can now look too all of you, as a meeting ready for a wedding. I would like to decorate your rooms with flowers and to start smiling again after thousands of years of darkness and helplessness.

Now your voices are stronger than the crowd who enslaved you and lied you. It is time to discover your power, to enjoy yourself freely of the pleasures of life, to be visionary and to stop complaining in the despair that encompassed the mankind.

So, lift-up and embrace knowledge!

Day 3

Why did I come to speak to you?

I look at you and become sad. I do not see joy, I do not hear laughter, but I answered those who searched for the truth, those who had the power to search, those who had the courage to build the pillars between the dead and the immortals, and these are my sons and my daughters.

Feel the joy and you will receive the answers to the mysteries of the universe.
Enjoy the fortunes, the gold, and the pleasures of life!
Smile! Everything is deep inside your soul!

Day 4

Those who love the pleasures, you know that you become angels through sex.
The strongest weapon of you has been taken and transformed into a sin. And you have closed your eyes and silently, as a sheep, you started to follow the mad man.
The nine weapons from inside of you have been turned into sins and you have no access to use them. Now is the time to dress them with ornaments of shine and to consider them as miraculous icons on the walls of your body. Yes, there is all within you, offered by God who created you according to his likeness.
Enter the pleasure house!
Oh, you who seek enlightenment and power, Come and don`t be afraid! Your heart can feel greatness and strength, and the power is now much clear, you can feel it. Everything is inside of you!

Day 5

Only those who want to know and feel with their heart will find the truth! Darkness and light create your universe.

We have stood for centuries and watched your decline, and we are watching your teachers and Emperors who are so pleased that you believe without asking, while they are enjoying the pleasures of life and guarding the truths.

You do not even have courage, now in this century, to step ahead and ask for the rights, for the truths and You... still believe in fairies and charming princes. Only a few of you have demonstrated that they deserve knowledge and is worth the gift of divine codes.

Day 6

We let the earth be driven by its own wires. We do not interfere!

Just as death defaults on life and spring breaks winter. We let everything differ in qualities and flaws. No one is equal to another.

On the mediocre creatures of the earth, let them eliminate each other, as well as their homes and their places. You sit silent and watch and you will find peace.

Those in our kingdom will choose those who deserve illumination and knowledge. Now you can be part of the change because your creator wants to be right. It's time to believe in yourself!

DAY 7

I am the knowledge!

And, I expect you, patient like a parent, to come to me and ask for my book. You will come after you will cry and suffer enough. Look around the mankind hate the life they live in. Everything has become a torture, pain, and distrust ...

and they call it "fate". Laughter, depression and hate between all this people will destroy everything around you.

What can you tell me about Ignorance?

Stay alone and look!

Do not try to convince anyone, because everyone has their own level of knowledge.

Carefully choose who you receive in your circle so that you do not regret it later that it has disturbed you and removed you from the path of enlightenment and peace.

Only those with the same thoughts and aspirations, vibrating on the same energy frequency, they can have access to your circle of friends.

Be very careful!

Day 8

The money

The money comes when your energy is a shiny gold light. We do not know the money here, you don`t need to beg God help you have money! We like the gold from the earth, money is just an energy, an illusion.

Yes, you must love money and gold! You have to love shopping, nice clothes, traveling, meeting new people, and discover new places. You must enjoy having beautiful homes, your favorite car, and what else do you want? When I want something I predict it, I give it a term, I accept it happily.

The Words and the heart are your strength!

Ask and you will have it!

Day 9

Say after me:

I am the Immortal Self

I step between light and darkness

I treasure my life, and your life, because I am a high creation of God.

I'm proud and I honor myself!

I acknowledge my mission and the truth,

I accept myself part of Light and Darkness, both together in my universe!

I only defend myself and respect all religions.

It is no hell or heaven, the only hell and heaven, exists only within me.

I live my life here and now!

I enjoy the pleasures of life and I will have everything I want.

I live in harmony with the universe!

How to Charge a Sigil and How to Use it

You have either been or at some point will be presented with certain "sigils" (symbolic representations of the outcomes of creative magic). Many are both aware of what to do and how to do when it is you do with sigils. Others however may meekly admit to requiring a bit of guidance to the ways of both charging a sigil and in how to use one in the course of their magic, in their meditations, or as representations symbolizing the power they wish to put forth before them.

Here in the following you will find a rather simple ritual, presented in step-by-step fashion, to help to give you some basic thrust forward along your way. This so-as-to free you to feel comfortable to move on as you will with your own style and way.

Many have or will reach the zenith of their own particular-way in what they do spiritually or magically so-as to do such rituals at their own specified points in time. One way that is popular is to charge a sigil at the power of the full moon. In the end, you will do as you will.

The Full Moon Charging of Your Sigil

- Once you have received your sigil, you may then wish to charge it with the vibration of your own magic, your own sense of creative spirit.

- At the evening of the full moon, prepare yourself and the quiet, private ceremonial area of your ritual.

- Gather and light your incense and set your altar pieces in their place.

- Once you have prepared yourself and feel cleansed and able to freely direct the force of your spirit upon your sigil commence with the following.

- Take the sigil and lay it upon your altar, or a clean cleansed flat surface.

- Commence with quieting yourself and centering your thoughts upon the God(s), Goddess(es), and spirits you are calling upon to render aid in charging your sigil with power and unwavering strength.

- Raising your hands in a way to beckon the God(s) to provide you with the channel of energy directed from the energy of the full moon into your sigil and say some form of the following according to your own ways of belief and following:

- "I ask beckon you (God(s) of your choice) to now provide me with the strength and power to invoke the energy of the full moon and that of the universe into this sigil I have laid before me"

• "In your presence and according to your will, I command that all of the force and energy of the full moon and of the universe lend itself to my will….. so be it, or, (so mote it be)".

• "I now humbly ask and I freely accept that this sigil is now to be a pure, a sure, and an unwavering symbol of my will and I accept and now choose to use its energy to work for me and to aid me in my ways. So be it, or, (so mote it be)".

• "Let this sigil now set my energy, to reveal to my mind and thoughts, to act upon my magic, that it will guide me and reveal all that is necessary to help me. So be it, or, (so mote it be)".

• Now close your eyes and focus all your mind and all of your thoughts upon the form and symbol of your sigil.

• Note every line and curve.

• In your mind picture the sigil as being alive, glowing in color, charged with the creative force of the universe. Picture your sigil as always being ready to aid you along your way.

• Now, meditate for a time on this.

• Once you feel you have completed the charging, open your eyes and bow your head and thank the God(s) and the universe for carrying this sigil to you.

• Silence your candles and your incense.

Your charging ritual is complete.

Remember, all sigils are ultimate symbols of power and of spirit and they all carry a presence that will never leave our consciousness or our spirit as we move onward.

This is in the nature of the sigil and the real presence of power of spirit that they provide to us as they always have since the earliest days in the dawning of humankind.

Be well in your ways!

The Sigils of the Devil

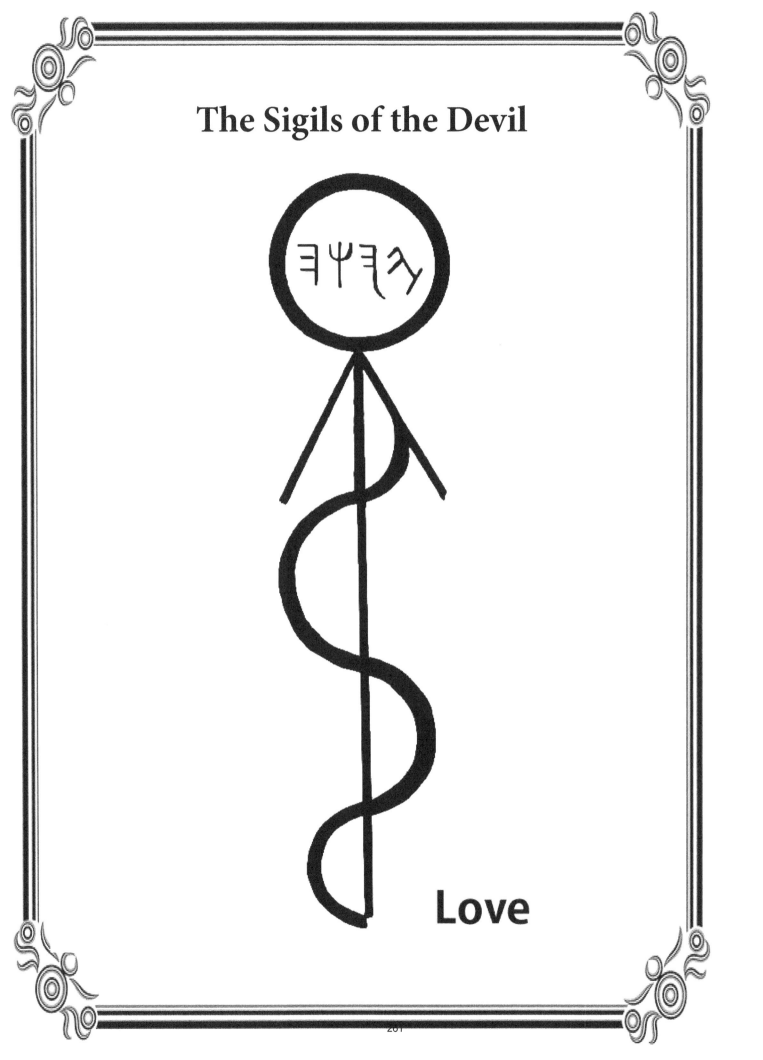

Love

Power

Prosperity

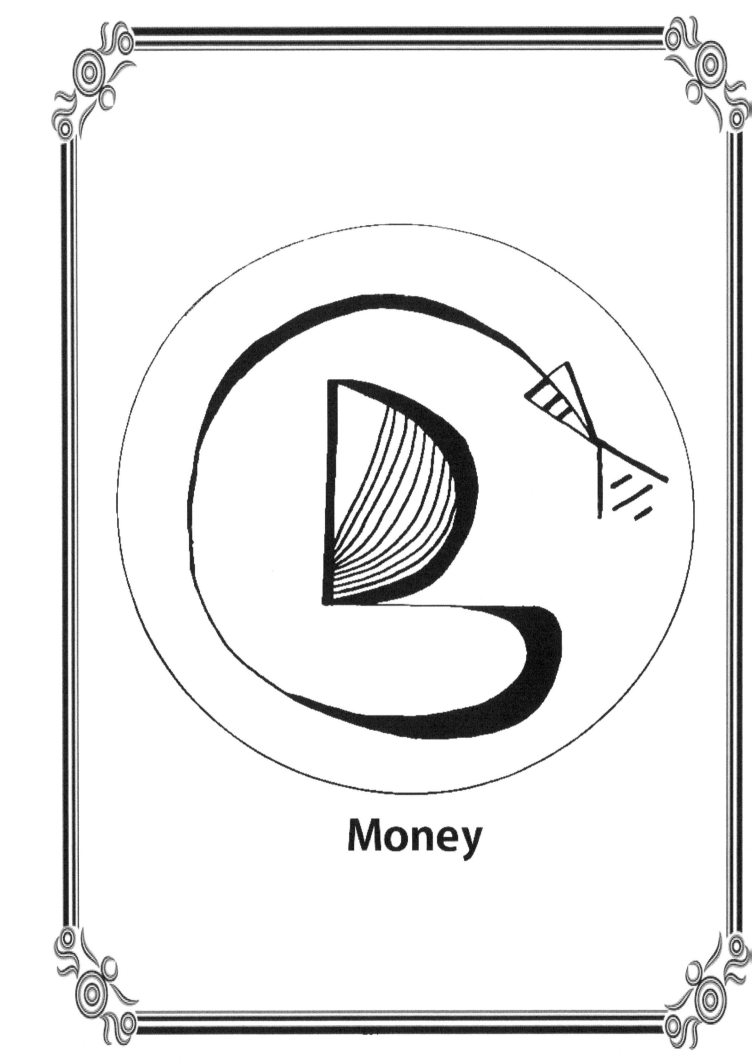

Money

Creation

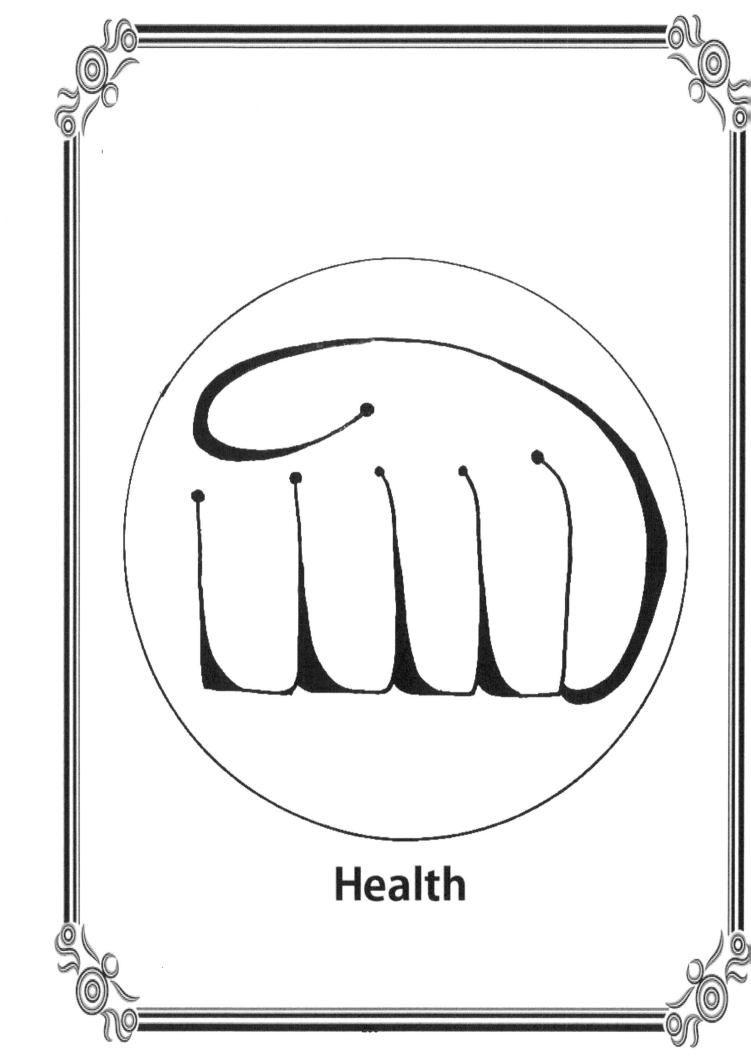

Health

The Undead

Calm Mind

NOTES

Made in the USA
Columbia, SC
14 June 2022

61751580R00154